D1318714

PHOTOGRAPHS
AND ILLUSTRATIONS
PRINTED
WITH PERMISSION

•

Library of Congress Catalog
Card Number: 91-076382

1791-1991

THE BILL OF RIGHTS

and Beyond

"THE SACRED RIGHTS OF MANKIND ARE NOT TO BE RUMMAGED FOR, AMONG OLD PARCHMENTS, OR MUSTY RECORDS.

"**THEY ARE WRITTEN, AS WITH A SUN BEAM IN THE WHOLE VOLUME OF HUMAN NATURE, BY THE HAND OF THE DIVINITY ITSELF, AND CAN NEVER BE ERASED OR OBSCURED BY MORTAL POWER.**"

—Alexander Hamilton

The Statue of Liberty represents the rights and the freedom of opportunity secured by the U. S. Constitution. On the statue's pedestal is the poem "The Colossus" by Emma Lazarus with the now-famous words, "Give me your tired, your poor, your huddled masses yearning to breathe free."

AMERICA HAS ALWAYS BEEN ABOUT RIGHTS.

We were the first people in history to found a nation on the basis of individual rights — a nation governed by "we the people." We have learned, not just by studying the "old parchments," but by living out their promise. While many nations are based upon a common religion or ethnic heritage, or upon natural geographic frontiers, Americans have made individual rights the foundation of our national identity.

We the people provided for a government instituted to provide order with liberty. Our Declaration of Independence offered the promise of such a government; the men who endured great hardships and suffering from Lexington to Valley Forge and Yorktown were not thinking about the details of a new national government or separation of powers, but they were fighting for the freedoms embodied in the ringing phrases of the Declaration of 1776. The Constitution and the Bill of Rights began to fulfill these promises by providing for a new system of government which the people controlled.

For those who sought our shores from many countries and cultures, America has remained the great land of opportunity with no aristocracy except for the aristocracy of achievement. Even our failures have been measured by the rights to which we aspire. Throughout our history, we have not always been successful in balancing the interests of the minority with the wishes of the majority. The promises of the new nation were not immediately extended to native Americans who were here first, or to African-Americans brought here against their will. But the struggle to right the wrongs has continued, and as Martin Luther King exhorted us, America has risen up "to live out the true meaning of its creed."

Americans have always believed, in the words of Henry Steele Commager, "that nothing in all history . . . ever succeeded like America." As it stands today, our Constitution and the Bill of Rights express the fundamental ideal of liberty, justice, and equality which have shaped the American experience, and have also made us a beacon to other peoples seeking a better life.

WARREN E. BURGER
Chairman, Commission on the Bicentennial
of the United States Constitution
Chief Justice of the United States, 1969-1986

Congress OF THE United States

begun and held at the City of New-York, on
Wednesday the Fourth of March, one thousand and seven hundred and eighty nine

THE Conventions of a number of the States, having at the time of their adopting the Constitution, expresse or abuse of its powers, that further declaratory and restrictive clauses should be added: And as extending the ground of public confidence in the Government, will best RESOLVED by the Senate and House of Representatives of the United States of America, in Congress concurring that the following Articles be proposed to the Legislatures of the several States, as amendments to the Constitution of the United States, all, or any of which said Legislatures, to be valid to all intents and purposes, as part of the said Constitution; viz.

ARTICLES in addition to, and Amendment of the Constitution of the United States of America, propos of the several States, pursuant to the fifth Article of the original Constitution.

Article the first..... After the first enumeration required by the first Article of the Constitution, there shall be one Representative for every thirty thousand, until the n which, the proportion shall be so regulated by Congress, that there shall be not less than one hundred Representatives, nor less than one until the number of Representatives shall amount to two hundred, after which the proportion shall be so regulated by Congress, that there shal nor more than one Representative for every fifty thousand persons.

Article the second.... No law, varying the compensation for the services of the Senators and Representatives, shall take effect, until an election of Representatives shall

Article the third..... Congress shall make no law respecting an establishment of religion, or prohibiting the free exercise thereof; or abridging the freedom of speech, or of the assemble, and to petition the Government for a redress of grievances.

Article the fourth.... A well regulated Militia, being necessary to the security of a free State, the right of the people to keep and bear Arms, shall not be infringe

Article the fifth...... No Soldier shall, in time of peace be quartered in any house, without the consent of the owner, nor in time of war, but in a manner to be pres

Article the sixth..... The right of the people to be secure in their persons, houses, papers, and effects, against unreasonable searches and seizures, shall not be viola probable cause, supported by Oath or affirmation, and particularly describing the place to be searched, and the persons or things to be seized

Article the seventh... No person shall be held to answer for a capital, or otherwise infamous crime, unless on a presentment or indictment of a Grand Jury, except in cases Militia, when in actual service in time of War or public danger; nor shall any person be subject for the same offence to be twice put in jeopardy criminal case to be a witness against himself, nor be deprived of life, liberty, or property, without due process of law; nor shall private prope

Article the eighth... In all criminal prosecutions, the accused shall enjoy the right to a speedy and public trial, by an impartial jury of the State and district whe district shall have been previously ascertained by law, and to be informed of the nature and cause of the accusation; to be confronted with the for obtaining witnesses in his favor, and to have the assistance of Counsel for his defence.

Article the ninth.... In suits at common law, where the value in controversy shall exceed twenty dollars, the right of trial by jury shall be preserved, and no fact tri any Court of the United States, than according to the rules of the common law.

Article the tenth..... Excessive bail shall not be required, nor excessive fines imposed, nor cruel and unusual punishments inflicted.

Article the eleventh. The enumeration in the Constitution, of certain rights, shall not be construed to deny or disparage others retained by the people

Article the twelfth.. The powers not delegated to the United States by the Constitution, nor prohibited by it to the States, are reserved to the States respectively

ATTEST,

Frederick Augustus Muhlenberg, Speaker of the House of Representative

John Adams, Vice President of the United States

John Beckley, Clerk of the House of Representatives.

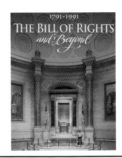

Contents

Two Virginians

Two Virginians, George Mason and James Madison, played major roles in the drama that created the Constitution and the Bill of Rights. Both favored a national government that would unify the country, and both firmly believed in personal rights. They differed, however, on how to attain these goals. Madison, an architect of the Constitution, believed that since the new federal government would be one of limited powers, authority not delegated to it would be retained by the people or the states.

Mason, author of the Virginia Declaration of Rights that inspired the federal Bill of Rights, also viewed the federal government as one of limited powers. He was concerned, however, that federal powers could erode those of the states. In a letter to his son, Mason voiced his anxiety, noting "there would be much difficulty in organizing a government upon this great scale and at the same time reserving to the state legislatures a sufficient portion of power for promoting and securing the prosperity and happiness of their respective citizens. . . ."

During the Federal Convention in Philadelphia in 1787, attended by both men as delegates from Virginia, Madison focused on the creation of a structure for a new federal government. Mason, on the other hand, softly but often brought up the question of rights during the debates. He reminded delegates to "attend to the rights of every class of the people."

VIRGINIA MUSEUM OF FINE ART

*"...no free government,
or the blessings of liberty,
can be preserved
to any people, but . . .
by frequent recurrence to
fundamental principles."*
GEORGE MASON

Mason discerned in the outlines of the proposed Constitution an enormous growth in the power of the federal government. He joined a small band of delegates to call for guarantees of personal liberties. Charles Pinckney of South Carolina proposed a list of important guarantees, some of which were incorporated into the Constitution.

Mason, who was still disenchanted, suggested a second convention to allow personal guarantees to be put into the Constitution. His followers, together with others who opposed the Constitution, became known as Anti-Federalists. Those who favored the proposed Constitution became known as Federalists.

Before the convention adjourned, Mason made a final plea for a bill of rights, and upon its rejection, he refused to sign the Constitution. He was joined by fellow Virginian Edmund Randolph and Massachusetts delegate Elbridge Gerry, who suspected that the new government would form a standing, professional army, "the bane of liberty from [the time of the] Roman legions. . . ."

The other 39 delegates present in Philadelphia on September 17, 1787, signed the Constitution. Most of the delegates did not totally embrace the document, but they thought it was better than nothing at all. The Constitution was sent to the states and the campaign began over ratification and a bill of rights.

Mason returned to Virginia an unhappy man. As Madison later reported to Jefferson, who was serving in Paris as America's minister to France, "Col. Mason left Philadelphia in an exceeding ill humor indeed. He returned to Virginia with a fixed disposition to prevent the adoption of the plan if possible. He considers the want of a Bill of Rights as a fatal objection."

The debate over ratification was carried out in state conventions and in the press. Both sides had brilliant advocates. *The Federalist Papers,* written by John Jay (the nation's first Chief Justice), Alexander Hamilton (the first Secretary of Treasury), and James Madison (the fourth President), are today considered among the world's finest writings on political theory.

The Anti-Federalists had eloquence and wisdom on their side as well. Mason wrote a series of essays called "Objections"; George Clinton of New York used the pen name "Cato" for his newspaper articles; and Melancton Smith wrote under the title of a "Federal Farmer." In Virginia the Anti-Federalists commanded a powerful weapon in the oratory and political following of Patrick Henry.

In *Federalist No. 84,* Hamilton pointed out that the body of the Constitution itself contained several provisions that secured individual rights. He cited the document's guarantee of jury trial and the right of habeas corpus, and its prohibition of bills of attainder, ex post facto laws, and titles of nobility, as well as its strict definition of treason.

Madison and others pointed out

"My own opinion has always been in favor of a bill of rights; provided it be so framed as not to imply powers not meant to be included in the enumeration. At the same time I have never thought the omission a material defect, nor been anxious to supply it even by subsequent amendment, for any other reason than that it is anxiously desired — by others."

JAMES MADISON

that by its very structure the Constitution precluded tyranny of the central government. Did not the Constitution's division of power between federal and state governments and its separation of powers among the three branches of government provide safeguards sufficient to protect against tyrants? Not only did the Federalists believe a bill of rights was unnecessary; some discovered a potential danger in including such a document in the Constitution. Any enumeration of fundamental rights might be too limiting, carrying with it the implication that any right not included did not exist. Moreover, as Hamilton asked, "Why declare that things shall not be done which there is no power to do? Why, for instance, should it be said, that the liberty of the press shall not be restrained, when no power is given by which restrictions may be imposed?"

Responding, the Anti-Federalists turned this argument on its head. If Hamilton were correct, weren't those rights already listed in the Constitution themselves in danger? For example, Anti-Federalists asked, is the right of trial by jury jeopardized because it is guaranteed by the Constitution?

The Federalists had the advantage of unity in their support of the Constitution and the Anti-Federalists were divided among themselves in their reasons for opposing. The call for a bill of rights, however, was the one agenda item on which the Anti-Federalists were agreed and it proved to be the most effective

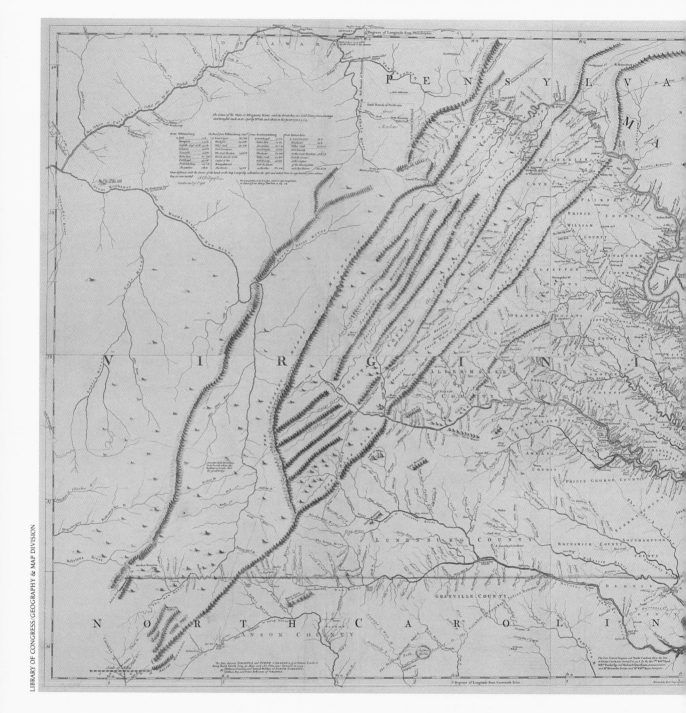

THE FRY-JEFFERSON MAP

created in 1751 "had no peer in the 18th century." It was revised in 1755
to include the system of roads developed in the colony as it expanded westward.
It was later reprinted by the French. West Virginia and Kentucky were
formed from parts of Virginia. The map, created by Joshua Fry, a professor
of mathematics at the College of William and Mary, and Peter Jefferson, a
surveyor and father of Thomas Jefferson, is in the Library of Congress collection.

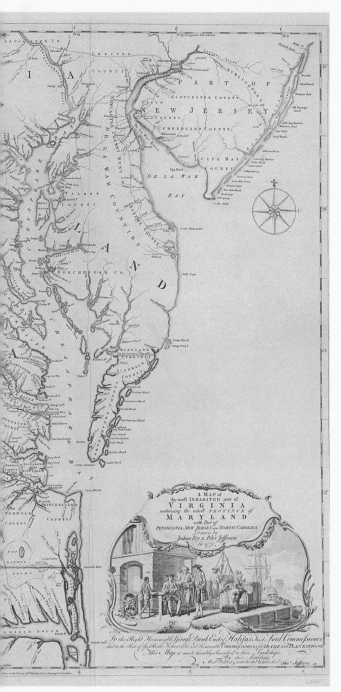

Dates of Interest to the History of the Bill of Rights*

*Britain and America used the old Julian Calendar until September 1752, when the Gregorian Calendar, already followed in most of Europe, was adopted. In the 18th century the latter calendar was 11 days "ahead" of the former. For example, March 16, 1751, is Madison's birthday on the Julian Calendar (March 27, 1751, on today's). Please note that most historical dates before 1752 that are listed in this and subsequent chapters follow the Julian Calendar.

June 15, 1215   The Magna Carta is signed.

November 11, 1620   The Mayflower Compact is signed, providing for a form of government based upon general agreement.

June 7, 1628   England's Charles I agrees to the Petition of Right.

January 14, 1639   Connecticut settlements enact the Fundamental Orders, providing for a plan of government based on popular consent; this document remains the basis of Connecticut's Constitution until 1818.

July 4, 1639   New Hampshire colonists sign the Exeter Compact, patterned after the Mayflower Compact.

July 9, 1640   The Netherlands issue a new Charter of Freedoms and Exemptions to facilitate Dutch colonization of New Amsterdam (later New York).

February 20, 1665   Proprietors of New Jersey present their Concessions and Agreements, providing for a representative assembly and liberty of conscience in the colony.

March 1, 1669   English proprietors of Carolina propose the Fundamental Constitutions, allowing for freedom of conscience; an amended version is enacted the following year.

March 3, 1677   *The Laws, Concessions, and Agreements* is published by the Proprietors and Freeholders of West Jersey; it provides for right of trial by jury and freedom of conscience.

April 2, 1683   William Penn's *Frame for Government,* providing for representative government, is issued for Pennsylvania and Delaware.

October 20, 1683   Delegates from New York, Maine, Nantucket, and Martha's Vineyard propose a Charter of Liberties, calling for representative government and taxation based on consent.

February 13, 1689   King William III and Queen Mary II agree to the English Bill of Rights.

June 9, 1732   A Royal charter, providing for freedom of conscience for all Protestants, is granted for the new colony of Georgia.

June 12, 1776   Virginia adopts what will become the first state bill of rights; it is called the Declaration of Rights.

July 13, 1787   The Northwest Ordinance is passed, banning slavery and securing freedom of conscience in the Northwest Territory.

September 17, 1787   The Constitution is signed by 39 men from the 12 states represented at the Convention; 3 delegates refuse to sign because of the omission of a bill of rights.

February 6, 1788   The Massachusetts ratification convention is the first to propose adding a bill of rights to the new Constitution, then ratifies the Constitution by a vote of 187-168.

May 4, 1789   Representative James Madison of Virginia proposes that debate in the first Congress on amendments to the Constitution begin at the end of the month.

September 25, 1789   The House and Senate agree on 12 proposed amendments to the Constitution and submit them to the states for ratification.

November 21, 1789   North Carolina, with a proposed bill of rights by Congress, ratifies the original Constitution by a 194 to 77 vote.

December 15, 1791   Virginia ratifies the Bill of Rights, making it part of the Constitution.

December 10, 1948   The U.N. General Assembly approves the U.N. Universal Declaration of Human Rights. The date is now commemorated worldwide as Human Rights Day.

December 15, 1952   The Constitution and the Declaration of Independence, having been moved from the Library of Congress, are put on permanent display with the Bill of Rights (which was moved from the State Department in September 1938) in the National Archives in Washington, D.C.

Montpelier: Home of James Madison, Orange County, Virginia.

weapon in their campaign against the ratification of the Constitution.

In the end, the Federalist arguments for omitting a bill of rights proved unconvincing. John Adams in London and Thomas Jefferson in Paris called on the Constitution's supporters to accept a bill of rights. Jefferson wrote, "a bill of rights is what the people are entitled to against every government on earth, general or particular, and what no just government should refuse or rest on inference."

The Federalists were forced to compromise. Beginning in Massachusetts in February 1788, the Constitution was ratified on the understanding that amendments providing a bill of rights would follow. When New Hampshire ratified on June 21, 1788, the Constitution

legally took effect. Without the endorsement of the larger states, however, no permanent union or government could be maintained. After nip-and-tuck struggles in their state conventions, New York and Virginia ratified in 1788 (by votes of 30-27 and 89-79, respectively). Virginia, with its ratification, proposed a list of amendments adapted from Mason's Declaration of Rights, and these provisions provided a basis for the federal Bill of Rights.

Steps were promptly taken to hold the election of members of Congress and a President. James Madison, who considered the Federalist commitment to a bill of rights as binding and was prepared himself to work on its behalf, was elected as a member of the new Congress from Virginia. Patrick Henry was successful in his

efforts to prevent Madison from winning a seat in the Senate. George Mason declined to run for the Senate.

In the first session of Congress, Madison introduced a proposed bill of rights. Beyond his determination to honor the commitments made during the struggle for ratification, Madison wanted to head off more radical changes in the Constitution, including calls for another constitutional convention. More than 200 different amendments had been proposed by the states. Madison narrowed these down to about two dozen. Many of the proposals from the states spoke in absolute or general terms. Madison's practical genius transformed these sweeping statements into a short list of specific restraints, consistent with the original Constitution. Instead of incorporating an outright ban on standing armies, for example, the proposed amendments provided for specific and practical limitations on the power of a professional military. Instead of saying that the government "ought not" to interfere with the liberty of the press, the eventual First Amendment said more explicitly that "Congress shall make no law . . . abridging" the same. Following debate in the House and the Senate, 12 amendments were passed by the Congress and sent to the states for ratification on September 25, 1789.

The first two amendments dealt with Congressional apportionment and pay and have never been ratified. Within six months, nine states had ratified the Bill of Rights. The admission of Vermont to the Union on March 4, 1791, made necessary the ratification by 11 states. Vermont ratified the amendments in November 1791, and Virginia once again held center stage. Though not all of the Anti-Federalists in that state were satisfied, Mason indicated the amendments gave him "much satisfaction," and on December 15, 1791, Virginia became the eleventh state to ratify the Bill of Rights, thus making it part of the Constitution. Its passage had a healing effect, giving as Mason had earlier predicted, "great quiet" to the people.

Yet Secretary of State Thomas Jefferson was matter-of-fact in the official notification of the adoption of the Bill of Rights he sent to state governors on March 1, 1792. After informing their excellencies of Congressional legislation concerning the nation's fisheries, post office, and post roads, he noted, almost as an afterthought, "also the ratifications by three fourths of the Legislatures of the Several States, of certain articles in addition and amendment to the Constitution of the United States, proposed by Congress to the said Legislatures. . . ."

After declining to run for the Senate, Mason retired from public life. In ill health, he died on October 7, 1792, at the age of 67. Madison became Secretary of State, and in 1808 he was elected President and served for two terms. He died on June 27, 1836, at the age of 85, the last surviving signer of the Constitution.

The legacies of these two great Virginians remain with us today. Madison offered the vision of an extended republic whose very diversity and division of power would assure limited government. Mason appealed to a tradition dating back to the Magna Carta, which maintained that certain fundamental rights transcended the power of any government, however constituted, to alter or abolish. Both legacies have shaped America's experiment in constitutional government. It is Mason's vision of fundamental rights, as carefully set into the Constitution by Madison's crafting, that we celebrate this year in the 200th anniversary of the Bill of Rights.

Gunston Hall: Home of George Mason, Fairfax County, Virginia.

The First Amendment

As much as any other single individual, Roger Williams set the stage for the religious freedom clause of the First Amendment. "A permission of the most Paganish, Jewish, Turkish, or Anti-Christian consciences and worships be granted to all men in all nations and countries," said Williams in a pamphlet penned to support his ideas on how to create and organize a colonial government.

Williams arrived in the New World from England in 1631. A Puritan minister of firm convictions, he felt the Pilgrims of Massachusetts Bay had not distanced themselves sufficiently from the Church of England. In a 1634 sermon Williams declared that "forced worship is false worship." Such statements did not set well with the Puritans of Salem, Massachusetts, who ran the New England colony as a theocracy, or church-controlled state.

In 1635 Williams was banished from the colony for life for his unorthodox beliefs. He fled to the south, and in an area that later became the colony of Rhode Island he built a wood cabin, which he named Providence. Williams secured a Royal Charter in 1644 for the colony. Following his Baptist beliefs, Williams insisted that its provisions include liberty of conscience for all citizens and a complete separation of church and state. As a result, Rhode Island became a haven for religious minorities — Roman Catholics, Jews, and Quakers — who suffered persecution in the other colonies at the time.

ROGER WILLIAMS
1603-1683

The First Amendment broke with the tradition in many countries that made one religion the established (official) church and supported it with government funds. It forbids Congress to set up or in any way provide for an established church. Congress also may not pass laws that limit the right to worship.

Freedom of conscience was one of the most dominant forces that drove people to seek refuge and freedom in America, beginning with the Pilgrims and the Puritans of the 17th century.

But many of the people who fled the conformity of "established" religions in the Old World to enjoy freedom to worship in the New World gave preferential status to their own faiths. Six American

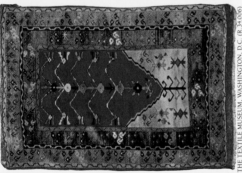

AMENDMENT I – CONGRESS SHALL MAKE NO LAW RESPECTING AN ESTABLISHMENT OF RELIGION, OR PROHIBITING THE FREE EXERCISE THEREOF. . . .

SITES EXHIBIT "MOSCOW TREASURES AND TRADITIONS"

THE TEXTILE MUSEUM, WASHINGTON, D.C. (R 34.006)

colonies maintained "established religions," and three others had favored denominations.

The colonists were not always tolerant of other faiths. The Puritans of New England intended to maintain their "garden of God" by keeping out non-Puritans. In 1631 the Massachusetts assembly ruled that "no man shall be admitted to the freedom of this body politic but such as are members of some of the churches within the limits of same."

Nonconformists, who disagreed with the established church, however, could move to new territories, and the Reverend Roger Williams did just that when he was banished from Massachusetts in

Religious diversity in America: a Christian triptych; an Islamic prayer rug; and a Jewish Hanukkah lamp (left).
Early Puritans of New England Going to Worship
by George Henry Boughton (below).

1635 because of unorthodox ideas. He fled to Rhode Island and founded the settlement of Providence. Religious freedom became the keystone of his new colony.

In 1663 Rhode Island became the first colony to provide for religious liberty in its Charter. The Charter said that "noe person . . . shall bee any wise molested, punished, disquieted, or called in question, for any differences in opinione in matters of religion." The free exercise clause of the First Amendment can be traced directly to Roger Williams and his Providence colony.

More than a century later George Mason drafted the Virginia Declaration of Rights, in 1776, calling for the "fullest toleration" of nonmembers of the established Anglican Church in that state.

James Madison, a Virginian and colleague of Mason's, and later the major force in the passage of the Bill of Rights through Congress, said that toleration was not the same as liberty, and Madison suggested that the Declaration read ". . . all men are equally entitled to enjoy the free exercise of religion." Mason agreed, aware of the strife that religious intolerance had caused in the Old World. Madison's stronger religious freedom language was used not only in the Virginia Declaration but also in the First Amendment.

Madison had come to believe that not mere toleration but complete equality in the right to worship was the surest guarantee of religious freedom because it allowed for a multiplicity of faiths. "If there were a majority of one sect," he said, "a bill of rights would be a poor protection for liberty."

The religion clause of the First Amendment has two parts. "Free exercise of religion" means that a person is free to practice any religion, and he is also free to choose not to practice religion and will not be persecuted or discriminated against because of his decision. When religious practice conflicts with a law that serves a legitimate, nonreligious purpose, however, the law has taken precedence.

For example, an 1862 law prohibiting polygamy in the Utah territory affected the religious practice of plural marriage by Mormons. In 1878 the Supreme Court upheld the law, noting that although "laws . . . cannot interfere with mere religious belief and opinions, they may with practices."

The amendment's other provision, the "establishment clause," ensured that the federal government would neither favor nor discriminate against any religious entity. In 1802, echoing Roger William's observation that there should be "a wall of separation between the garden of the Church and the wilderness of the world," Thomas Jefferson wrote that the intention of the First Amendment was to build a "wall of separation between church and state."

The first interpretation of the establishment clause came in 1811, when President Madison vetoed a bill in which Congress would have granted to Baptists land worth $10 in the Mississippi Territory to be used as a meetinghouse. In his veto message, President Madison said, "the bill . . . comprises a principle and precedent . . . contrary to the article of the Constitution which declares that

JOHN T. HOPF

Touro Synagogue, Newport, Rhode Island, dedicated in 1763, is the oldest Jewish temple in America (left).
Religious freedom: symbols of some of the many religions in the United States (l. to r.): Bahai, Buddhist, Christian, Hindu (top), Islam, Jain, Jewish, Sikh (bottom).

June 1636   Roger Williams founds Providence, Rhode Island, as a haven of religious toleration.

May 24, 1689   The English Parliament passes the Act of Toleration, granting freedom of worship to Protestants.

May 1692   Salem witch trials begin in Massachusetts.

1728   Jewish colonists erect first American synagogue in New York City.

December 24, 1784   James Madison publishes his *Remonstrances Against Religious Assessments,* advocating separation of church and state.

January 16, 1786   The Virginia House of Burgesses passes the Statute of Religious Freedom, abolishing an established church in Virginia.

August 15, 1790   Father John Carroll is consecrated as the first Roman Catholic Bishop of the United States.

November 11, 1833   Massachusetts becomes the last state to withdraw tax support of an established church.

June 30, 1864   "In God We Trust" first appears on U.S. coinage.

January 6, 1879   The Supreme Court in *Reynolds v. United States* upholds the right of Congress to forbid polygamy in U.S. territories.

June 17, 1963   The Supreme Court rules in *Abington School District v. Schempp* that required reading from the Bible or of the Lord's Prayer was unconstitutional.

May 15, 1972   The Supreme Court rules in *Wisconsin v. Yoder* that a state may not require attendance at a formal high school where such attendance conflicts with the interests of a particular religion.

Congress shall make no law respecting a religious establishment."

Until the middle of the 20th century, the federal government allowed the states great latitude in dealing with matters of religion. In recent years, however, Supreme Court rulings have extended the establishment clause to the states under the Fourteenth Amendment and have, as a result, addressed a number of difficult issues, from the display of a Christmas creche and a Jewish menorah on public property to the use of public funds for sectarian school textbooks and remedial education.

Court rulings on religious issues have not been easy in the history of the First Amendment. The freedom it guarantees has sometimes given rise to a tension between profoundly held religious beliefs and the constitutional safeguards designed to ensure that freedom. Yet, these safeguards have not only allowed the deepest of religious convictions to flourish; they have created a nation of diverse faiths on which that freedom may ultimately depend. James Madison expressed it best more than 200 years ago when he said that the diversity of religious belief "which pervades America is the best and only security for religion. . . ."

The First Amendment

he trial of John Peter Zenger was a harbinger of First Amendment rights. In 1735 the governor of New York ordered that charges of seditious libel be brought against Zenger, the publisher of the *New York Weekly Journal,* a colonial newspaper. Zenger had published a series of articles, written by others, highly critical of the government. The libel charge discounted the truth of the defendant's statements. Moreover, following current practice, the jury was only allowed to decide on whether Zenger was, in fact, the publisher of the articles — something he freely admitted. It was up to the judge of the case to decide the matter of libel.

Andrew Hamilton, Zenger's lawyer, and one of the great legal advocates of the day, argued, however, that the jury, like the press, was a "bastion of popular liberty." Therefore, it should decide the truthfulness of the newspaper columns, and it should have the power to return a libel verdict based solely on the accuracy of the articles. The judge, on the other hand, gave specific instructions limiting the jury to the question of Zenger's association with the newspaper. The jury ignored the judge's instructions and returned a verdict of "not guilty," taking upon itself to decide the law as well as the facts of the case. Hamilton later praised the jury: "You have laid a noble foundation for securing to ourselves that to which Nature and the Laws of our country have given us a Right — The Liberty — both of exposing and opposing arbitrary Power by speaking and writing Truth."

JOHN PETER ZENGER
1697-1746

ILLINOIS BORN UNDER THE ORDINANCE OF '87.

"WESTWARD THE STAR OF EMPIRE TAKES ITS WAY:
THE GIRLS LINK ON TO LINCOLN,
THEIR MOTHERS WERE FOR CLAY."

ABE
THE
GIANT-KILLER

THE
LITTLE GIANT
CHAWING UP
OLD ABE

BEALE Fct.

Senatorial candidates Stephen Douglas and Abraham Lincoln exercised freedom of speech in a historic series of election debates (left). From twenty-five cent newspapers to multi-million dollar television programs, the American media enjoy the freedom to inform, entertain, and educate (above).

LIBRARY OF CONGRESS. PHOTO REED BAKER

*F*irst Amendment rights of freedom of speech and of press guarantee citizens access to information needed to meet civic responsibilities. People must have freedom to communicate their ideas and to promote their views because only informed and involved citizens can make the American system of representative government work.

The First Amendment guarantees of freedom of speech and of the press resulted from a long struggle in British and American history. For centuries it had been a crime to criticize the king or his government, and critics suffered many injustices. Freedom of the press was controlled through licensing acts authorizing censors to seize unapproved books, and unlicensed printing presses were "melted, sawed in pieces, broken or battered" and scrap was returned to the print shop owner. Authors of unauthorized books were also subject to punishment.

In 1694 Parliament allowed the infamous Licensing Act and its censorship to lapse. The law of seditious libel, however, remained in effect. This law held writers and publishers accountable for any publication that bred disaffection with the government or subjected it to hatred and contempt, without regard to the truth or falsehood of the charges. In 1763 the law was used to deprive John Wilkes of his seat in the House of Commons after he was charged with seditious libel for publishing outspoken tracts against the king and his ministers. When Wilkes eventually prevailed against the charges and won back his seat, his defense of freedom of the press electrified the public imagination both in England and in America where the seditious libel acts also applied.

America found her own freedom of the press hero in John Peter Zenger, publisher of the *New York Weekly Journal*. Zenger was charged in 1735 with seditious libel for publishing articles criticizing an action of the royal governor. Zenger's attorney argued the truth of Zenger's publication was a defense against the charge of seditious libel. Despite the judge's direction to the jury to disregard this evidence, the jury acquitted Zenger.

When the colonies declared their independence from England and developed their own constitutions, eight of the 13 states included freedom of the press guarantees in their constitutions.

Freedom of the press as understood by the states (and by the Framers of the Constitution) meant no prior restraint upon any publication. Writers and publishers were still held accountable, however, for the consequences of their publications, i.e., published matter found to be libelous, seditious, obscene, or otherwise unacceptable at law.

In 1798 Congress enacted a Sedition Act, which made it a crime to utter, write, or publish anything "with intent to defame . . . or bring into contempt or disrepute" the President and other members of the government. The Act, designed to suppress criticism of the Federalist party, did, however, liberalize the well-established law of seditious libel by allowing the truth of whatever was expressed as a defense, thus confirming the victory of John Peter Zenger. The Act expired in 1801, and President Jefferson pardoned those who had been its victims.

When James Madison led the Bill of Rights in its passage through Congress, he wanted the rights of free speech and the press to apply to the states as well as to the federal government. The Senate, however, removed language that would have made the First Amendment binding on the states. Madison was dismayed and said that the Senate had cut "the most valuable amendment in the whole lot." Madison's vision became reality only in this century, through judicial construction of the Fourteenth Amendment.

Even some of the most ardent advocates of free speech accept the fact that this freedom is sometimes in tension with other social values. Defining the limits of freedom of expression has not been easy. Over the years, three main areas have evolved in which speech is not permitted absolute freedom in the face of other social values. The first is where speech inflicts injury on individuals (libel and slander). The second is where speech endangers public safety or the security of the government itself. The last has to do with instances of obscenity thought to undermine community moral values and therefore not accorded the constitutional protections of freedom of expression.

The First Amendment cases that reach the Supreme Court are often controversial because they involve troubling issues like criticism of public officials, the publication of books that contain offensive material, or forms of expression like flag burning.

Almost 200 years ago, John Marshall, "the Great Chief Justice," recognized the dilemma that the country and the courts would face in trying to define the boundaries of free speech and of the press. Marshall said, "That this [press] liberty is often carried to excess; that it has sometimes degenerated into licentiousness, is seen and lamented, but the remedy has not yet been discovered." He added that perhaps licentiousness "is an evil inseparable from the good with which it is allied; perhaps it is a shoot which cannot be stripped from the stalk without wounding vitally the plant from which it is torn."

HARLEE LITTLE, JR.

Presses print millions of words daily free of censorship or government control (above). A seditious libel trial based on a 1733 "Letter to the Editor" in Peter Zenger's newspaper vindicated freedom of the press (right).

Numb. 11.

THE

New - York Weekly JOURNAL

Containing the freſheſt Advices, Foreign, and Domeſtick.

MUNDAY November 12, 1733.

Mr. Zenger,

INcert the following in your next, and you'll oblige your Friend,
CATO.

Mira'temporum felicitas ubi ſentiri que velis, & que ſentias dicere licit.
Tacit.

THE Liberty of the Preſs is a Subject of the greateſt Importance, and in which every Individual is as much concern'd as he is in any other Part of Liberty: therefore it will not be improper to communicate to the Publick the Sentiments of a late excellent Writer upon this Point, ſuch is the Elegance and Perſpicuity of his Writings, that it will be difficult to ſay any Thing new that he has not ſaid, or not to ſay that much worſe which he has ſaid.

There are two Sorts of Monarchies, an abſolute and a limited one. In the firſt, the Liberty of the Preſs can never be maintained, it is inconſiſtent with it; for what abſolute Monarch would ſuffer any Subject to animadvert on his Actions, when it is in his Power to declare the Crime, and to nominate the Puniſhment? This would make it very dangerous to exerciſe ſuch a Liberty. Beſides the Object againſt which thoſe Pens ſmuſt be directed, is

their Sovereign, the ſole ſupream Magiſtrate; for there being no Law in thoſe Monarchies, but the Will of the Prince, it makes it neceſſary for his Miniſters to conſult his Pleaſure, before any Thing can be undertaken: He is therefore properly chargeable with the Grievances of his Subjects, and what the Miniſter there acts being in Obedience to the Prince, he ought not to incur the Harred of the People; for it would be hard to impute that to him for a Crime, which is the Fruit of his Allegiance, and for refuſing which he might incur the Penalties of Treaſon. Beſides, in an abſolute Monarchy, the Will of the Prince being the Law, a Liberty of the Preſs to complain of Grievances would be complaining againſt the Law, and the Conſtitution, to which they have ſubmitted, or have been obliged to ſubmit; and therefore, in one Senſe, may be ſaid to deſerve Puniſhment. So that under an abſolute Monarchy, I ſay, ſuch a Liberty is inconſiſtent with the Conſtitution, having no proper Subject in Politics, on which it might be exerciſ'd, and if exerciſ'd would incur a certainPenalty.

But in a limited Monarchy, as England is, our Laws are known, fixed, and eſtabliſhed. They are the ſtreight Rule and ſureGuide to direct the King, the Miniſters, and other his Subjects: And therefore an Offence againſt the Laws is ſuch an Offence againſt the Conſtitution as ought to receive a proper adequate Puniſhment; the levera Conſtil

CULVER PICTURES, INC.

November 25, 1644 John Milton publishes *Areopagitica* in defense of freedom of the press.

1694 The Licensing Act in England expires, ending official prior restraint on the press.

April 24, 1704 The *Boston News-Letter* becomes the first regularly issued newspaper in the colonies.

August 8, 1735 John Peter Zenger is acquitted by a jury of the charge of seditious libel.

June–July 1798 Congress passes the Alien and Sedition Acts, placing new limits on freedom of speech.

March 10, 1919 The Supreme Court in *Schenk v. United States* invokes the principle of "clear and present danger" to justify government suppression of the press.

June 8, 1925 The Supreme Court says in *Gitlow v. New York* that guarantees of freedom of speech in the First Amendment apply to the states through the Fourteenth Amendment.

June 1, 1931 The Supreme Court in *Near v. Minnesota* declares "prior restraint" unconstitutional, thus limiting censorship of newspapers and magazines before publication.

June 3, 1940 The Supreme Court upholds the power of the state to require the salute of the Pledge of Allegiance in the case of children whose parents had objected because of religious beliefs. Three years later, on June 14, 1943, the Supreme Court reverses itself in *West Virginia Board of Education v. Barnette*.

March 9, 1964 The Supreme Court rules in *New York Times v. Sullivan* that actual malice must be proved in libel suits involving public officials.

June 11, 1990 The Supreme Court rules in *Texas v. Johnson* that flag burning represents a form of symbolic speech and is therefore protected by the First Amendment.

The First Amendment

The First Amendment "right of the people peaceably to assemble, and to petition the government for a redress of grievances" might best be exemplified by the life and actions of the Reverend Dr. Martin Luther King, Jr. On August 28, 1963, before 250,000 people who had joined him in a "March on Washington for Jobs and Freedom," King proclaimed his vision for a new America, "I have a dream that my four little children will one day live in a nation where they will not be judged by the color of their skin, but by the content of their character."

A lifelong admirer of Indian leader Mohandas K. Gandhi and his philosophy of nonviolent resistance, Dr. King believed that a cornerstone demand of the civil rights movement was the right of all Americans peaceably to assemble in all public places. He led civil disobedience campaigns to desegregate public facilities and led numerous marches and protests. Arrested on 19 occasions, Dr. King, in his historic "Letter from a Birmingham Jail," defended his policies of nonviolent direct action and of criticizing those who acquiesced in racial segregation.

Dr. King had been propelled into the leadership of the civil rights movement in 1955 when he led a successful boycott of the Montgomery, Alabama, bus system. In 1964 Dr. King accepted the Nobel Peace Prize, whereupon he dedicated himself not only to the civil rights movement in America, but to the search for peace throughout the world. His assassination in 1968 made him a martyr to his cause.

NATIONAL PORTRAIT GALLERY, © BENEDICT J. FERNANDEZ

MARTIN LUTHER KING, JR.
1929-1968

The freedoms to assemble peaceably and to petition for the redress of grievances have been central to the American experience. The United States was born when representatives of various colonies joined together "in General Congress assembled" in 1776, first to petition for the redress of grievances against Great Britain and eventually to declare independence.

Historically, the rights to assemble and to petition have gone hand in hand. The first great charter of English liberties, the Magna Carta of 1215, was, in fact, a petition addressed to the king by certain of his subjects demanding confirmation of certain liberties. So, too, was the second great charter, the English Petition of Right of 1628. The English Bill of Rights of 1689 once more confirmed that "it is the right of the subjects to petition the king, and all commitments and prosecutions for such petitions are illegal."

The American colonists were well aware of this constitutional heritage and considered these rights as their own. Because the colonies had no representation in Parliament, petitioning the king and Parliament was the major way in which the colonies represented their views and grievances to the mother country. When the government ignored these legitimate grievances, frustration set in, leading to revolution.

In 1772 colonists in Massachusetts circulated the *Boston Pamphlet,* which complained that the royal governor had thwarted local government by adjourning assemblies "when important concerns of the province required their meeting." Colonists also complained that the agents paid to represent them in London had to be acceptable to the royal governor, "and we very well know what the man must be to whose appointment, a governor in such circumstances, will consent," said the *Boston Pamphlet.*

When the colonists met in the Stamp Act Congress of 1765 to demand a repeal of that hated tax, delegates issued a Declaration of Rights and Grievances, which said "that it is the right of the British subjects in these colonies to petition the king or either house of Parliament." With events moving toward a final rupture, the First Continental Congress met in 1774 to deal with the Coercive Acts, which had curtailed many activities of local government.

The Continental Congress issued a Declaration of Resolves, including the charge that "assemblies have been frequently

AMENDMENT I – CONGRESS SHALL MAKE NO LAW . . . ABRIDGING . . . THE RIGHT OF THE PEOPLE PEACEABLY TO ASSEMBLE, AND TO PETITION THE GOVERNMENT FOR A REDRESS OF GRIEVANCES.

ROBERT KELLY, LIFE MAGAZINE

During the 1963 "March on Washington,"
Dr. King delivered his inspiring speech, "I Have a Dream" (left).
Freedom of assembly and petition join with freedom of speech
in Norman Rockwell's painting, Town Meeting *(right).*

dissolved, contrary to the rights of the people, when they attempted to deliberate on grievances; and their dutiful, humble, loyal, and reasonable petitions to the crown for redress have been repeatedly treated with contempt, by his majesty's ministers of state. . . ."

The Second Continental Congress met on May 15, 1776, and concluded that since Britain had given "no answer, whatever, to the humble petition of the colonies . . . it is necessary that the exercise of every kind of authority under said crown should be totally suppressed. . . ."

Compromise and resolution seemed beyond reach, and the colonies declared their independence on July 4, 1776, with a Declaration listing abuses by the British crown. The Declaration said in part that "He [George III] has dissolved representative houses repeatedly, for opposing, with manly firmness his invasions on the rights of the people . . . in every stage of these oppressions we have petitioned for redress . . . answered only by repeated injury."

When the First Congress under the Constitution debated the Bill of Rights in 1789, Rep. Theodore Sedgwick argued that the proposed assembly and petition clause was "trifling" when compared with other rights. Rep. John Page of Virginia disagreed, saying that if people could be deprived "of the power of assembling under any pretext whatsoever, they might be deprived of every other privilege" in the First Amendment.

Originally, the right to assemble peaceably was considered less important than the right of petition. But as the courts have interpreted the First Amendment over the past two centuries, the right of assembly has acquired a fundamental importance of its own. These two rights have afforded protection for many reform movements, from the abolitionists before the Civil War to the suffrage cause in later decades to the civil rights struggle of recent years. These rights have also nurtured American labor in its long struggle to create unions and to undertake collective bargaining.

Even when the turmoil of the Vietnam War era severely tested the limits of these rights of assembly and petition, the nation's courts went to great lengths to protect them. The courts have also invoked the First Amendment to secure the right of public employees to participate in political life and the ability of all citizens to participate fully in the electoral process. For example, several court decisions in recent years have curtailed the government's ability to impose special limitations on which candidates and parties may participate.

A century and a half ago, Alexis de Tocqueville, the French observer of American life, commented on the remarkable inclination of Americans to form voluntary associations to solve common problems. From the beginning, the free speech, assembly, and petition guarantees of the First Amendment have helped to assure an informed and engaged citizenry on which the success of the Founders' experiment in republican government would depend.

Bostonians gather to protest the 1765 Stamp Act imposed by the British to raise money for British troops in the colonies (above). An 1841 petition from 182 citizens of Ohio asked Congress to reduce expenses because of the "general depreciation of property and labor" in the country (right).

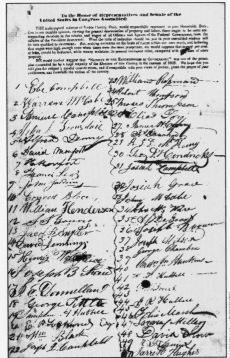

May 24, 1764   Opposition to Britain begins in Boston to protest the Stamp Act; James Otis denounces "taxation without representation."

July, 1765   Spurred by widespread opposition to the Stamp Act, a number of underground organizations calling themselves the "Sons of Liberty" are formed in various colonial towns.

September 5, 1774   First Continental Congress meets in Philadelphia.

February 11, 1790   The Society of Friends presents to Congress the first petition calling for the abolition of slavery.

May 26, 1836   The House of Representatives adopts a "gag" resolution declaring that all petitions and papers that in any way involve the issue of slavery should be set aside with no discussion. The resolution remains in place until 1844.

November 15, 1881   The American Federation of Labor is founded. The Congress of Industrial Organizations is founded on November 16, 1938; the two organizations merge to form the AFL-CIO on December 5, 1955.

May–June, 1932   The "Bonus March" on Washington is held.

January 4, 1937   The Supreme Court declares in *De Jonge v. State of Oregon* that the conviction of Communists for peaceable assembly is unlawful.

August 28, 1963   During a civil rights march on Washington, D.C., Martin Luther King, Jr., delivers his "I Have a Dream" speech.

March 7–25, 1965   Civil rights march from Selma to Montgomery, Alabama, takes place.

25

The Second and Third Amendments

One of the most outspoken critics of the original Constitution and an eloquent advocate for the Bill of Rights was Elbridge Gerry of Massachusetts. In debating the necessity of the Second Amendment, which gave militia the power to arm themselves, some delegates responded that militia were worthless as military forces. Gerry replied, "What, sir, is the use of a militia? It is to prevent the establishment of a standing army, the bane of liberty."

Gerry was active in the 1787 Constitutional Convention, yet when the time came for signing the Constitution, Gerry refused — one of only three delegates to do so. Gerry felt the Constitution had two serious deficiencies: it lacked a bill of rights to secure the liberties of the citizens, and the central government possessed too much military power.

Today, Gerry is remembered for backing a Congressional redistricting technique to keep his party in power, the "gerrymander." Early America remembered him, however, as a staunch defender of states' rights and personal liberties. John Adams once wrote of him, "If every man here was a Gerry, the liberties of America would be safe against the Gates of Earth and Hell."

ELBRIDGE GERRY
1744-1814

26

An ancient fear of being disarmed and helpless before standing professional armies lies behind the Second and Third Amendments. Aristotle said that decisions of a leader "backed by a standing army" would be different from those made by a leader "awed by the fear of an armed people." Niccolo Machiavelli wrote that the citizen-warrior was the strength of a republic and that armed citizens kept rulers honest. Not only did standing armies give government unbridled power, but the presence of a professional soldiery was often imposed upon ordinary citizens — for example, when housed among the people without their consent.

The experience of Britain and America in the conflicts of the 17th and 18th centuries created a deep-seated fear of standing armies and the threat that occupying armies posed to the rights of the civilian population. The rule of Oliver Cromwell's generals in England after the civil war of the 1640s and the attempt of King James II to "overawe" the nation in the 1680s led to a provision in the English Bill of Rights of 1689 that declared "raising of a standing army, unless with the consent of Parliament, is against the law."

One of the consequences of a standing army was the imposition of soldiers in the homes of civilians against their will. The English Petition of Right of 1628 complained that "great companies of soldiers and mariners have been dispersed into divers counties of the realm, and the inhabitants against their wills have been compelled to receive them into their houses. . . ."

As a result of the overthrow of James II and the creation of the Bill of Rights of 1689, the power of the crown to raise and deploy military forces was severely curtailed during the 18th century. Britain's failure to apply the same restraints in dealing with the American colonists helped lead to the American Revolution.

When relations between Britain and the American colonies worsened following the 1773 Boston Tea Party, Britain faced a citizenry armed and ready to defend its rights. In an effort to put down colonial unrest Britain imposed a series of laws called the Coercive Acts, which included the detested Quartering Act. It fed ancient fears of billeting a standing army among civilians.

The Quartering Act authorized colonial governors to open uninhabited buildings for the use of soldiers whenever they saw fit. Violating the sanctity of private property, the Act seemed a prelude to martial law and the imposition by force of British rule on colonies that had enjoyed substantial self-government for over 100 years. The reaction to these repressive acts was recorded in a series of pamphlets. Reminding Britain of its own hard-won Bill of Rights, the *Boston Pamphlet* of 1772 said "introducing and quartering standing armies in a free country in times of peace without the consent of the people . . . is, and always has been deemed a violation of their rights as freemen. . . ."

AMENDMENT II – A WELL REGULATED MILITIA, BEING NECESSARY TO THE SECURITY OF A FREE STATE, THE RIGHT OF THE PEOPLE TO KEEP AND BEAR ARMS, SHALL NOT BE INFRINGED.

AMENDMENT III – NO SOLDIER SHALL, IN TIME OF PEACE BE QUARTERED IN ANY HOUSE, WITHOUT THE CONSENT OF THE OWNER, NOR IN TIME OF WAR, BUT IN A MANNER TO BE PRESCRIBED BY LAW.

CONNECTICUT HISTORICAL SOCIETY

On April 19, 1775, an armed militia of farmers and tradesmen challenged professional British troops, as recorded by Amos Doolittle in an engraving called Battle of Lexington (above). The Minuteman statue honors the farmer-fighters of Concord-Lexington and the "shot heard round the world" for independence (right).

28

BY THE RUDE BRIDGE THAT
ARCHED THE FLOOD,
THEIR FLAG TO APRIL'S
BREEZE UNFURLED,
HERE ONCE THE EMBATTLED
FARMERS STOOD,
AND FIRED THE SHOT HEARD
ROUND THE WORLD.

Following independence in 1776, several of the colonies either converted their colonial charters into state constitutions or wrote new constitutions. Many of these new constitutions contained a bill of rights prohibiting a standing army and reaffirming the right of the states to raise a militia and the right of citizens to bear arms.

However, these provisions were not fully reflected in the new federal Constitution. The Framers shared the people's apprehension of a standing army and provided that Congressional appropriations for the army could last no more than two years at a time. Many were not satisfied, however, with this limitation. The states feared that the authority of the new national government to "raise and support" armies (Article I, Section 8) might signal the end of the state militia and citizens' rights to bear arms.

Madison maintained that state militia would serve as a counterbalance to any national armed forces. He argued in *Federalist No. 45* that a "regular army" in the service of the federal government would be no match for the combined militia of the states, "officered by men chosen from among themselves, fighting for their common liberties. . . ." He also wrote that the Constitution would not prohibit citizens from owning guns. Americans had the unique advantage of the right to bear arms, he said, and this right "forms a barrier against any enterprises of ambition. . . ."

The Anti-Federalists remained wary of the powers of Congress. Five of the eight states that proposed amendments to the Constitution wanted an amendment specifically authorizing the individual states to maintain a militia, prohibiting the quartering of troops, and reaffirming the right of citizens to bear arms.

One of the strongest opponents of a standing army was the Anti-Federalist Elbridge Gerry of Massachusetts. In a pamphlet, he wrote, "Standing armies have been the nursery of vice and the bane of liberty from the Roman legions . . . to the planting of the British cohorts in the capitals of America."

Both Samuel Adams, then governor of Massachusetts, and Thomas Jefferson advised Madison to include in his proposed amendments the right to bear arms. Adams coupled his recommendation with a caution against raising a standing army, even though the Constitution had authorized such a force.

Although the outright ban on standing armies that the Anti-Federalists had wished for was not included in the Constitution, the Second and Third Amendments provided practical checks on the dangers of military tyranny. These amendments were framed at a time when soldiers in other nations could be camped in private homes, kings could confiscate arms, and local citizens could be left defenseless and unable to secure their livelihood by hunting game. The ideal of the self-armed citizen had become well entrenched in American life long before the Minutemen stood at Lexington Green.

Throughout most of its history, America has had a professional army. The Constitution's provisions for civilian control of the

> "... in a constitutional government, those who possess arms are the citizens."
> ARISTOTLE

> "He [George III] has kept among us, in times of peace, standing armies without the consent of our Legislatures. ..."
> DECLARATION OF INDEPENDENCE

The Boston Massacre *engraving by Paul Revere helped convince citizens of the need to have the "right to bear arms."*

military, however, have meant that the worst fears of standing armies have never been realized, and the provisions of the Third Amendment have never been tested. The Second Amendment's endorsement of citizens' militia has been vindicated. State militia and National Guard units continue to play a vital role in the defense of the nation and in times of natural disaster. The Second Amendment prohibition of any infringement by the federal government of the fundamental right "to bear arms" has not prevented either the federal or state government from regulating the use of certain firearms (concealed weapons, for example) and prohibiting altogether the use of others (such as sawed-off shotguns and sub-machine guns). Recently, however, the meaning and scope of the Second Amendment have come under closer scrutiny in the light of urgent social problems involving crime and the use of firearms.

1608   First American militia formed in Jamestown Colony.

February 13, 1689   English Bill of Rights secures the rights of a "Protestant" militia.

March 24, 1765   Parliament passes the Quartering Act for British troops in the American colonies. In August 1766, New York citizens refuse to comply.

March 5, 1770   The "Boston Massacre" takes place.

June 2, 1774   Parliament amends 1765 Quartering Act to apply throughout the colonies.

October 5, 1774   Massachusetts initiates plans to organize a colonial militia, including the Minutemen.

August 6, 1824   The name "National Guard" is first applied to a state militia in New York.

November 1871   The National Rifle Association is incorporated.

June 26, 1934   The National Firearms Act, the first federal legislation regulating sale and use of firearms, is passed.

31

The Fourth Amendment

Protection of a citizen's home and belongings from unwarranted search and seizure by the government had no better champion than James Otis, a prominent colonial lawyer who felt government should not be allowed arbitrary or absolute power. In 1761 Otis asked the Massachusetts Superior Court to discontinue issuing writs of assistance, which allowed British customs agents, at their discretion, to search all houses suspected of harboring arms, contraband, or seditious documents.

Appealing to the court to base its decision on a "higher law," Otis argued that "the judges of England have declared . . . that acts of Parliament against natural equity are void." In his opinion, the writs violated natural law by giving police unlimited powers of search and seizure throughout an entire area. He tried unsuccessfully to convince the court that it held the power of judicial review over acts of Parliament.

The publicity of the case, however, was such that most colonial courts subsequently refused to issue such writs, and later eight states explicitly inserted guarantees against general warrants in their constitutions. The Bill of Rights prohibited general warrants because the public mood was so against them.

Although Otis always denied the revolutionary nature of his writings, his briefs were later used by Alexander Hamilton to support the concept of judicial review.

JAMES OTIS
1725-1783

The association between liberty and property has roots deep in the American and English past. Through the centuries, champions of human rights saw the right to acquire and hold property as fundamental because it secured life and liberty as well. The great English statesman and friend of American rights, William Pitt, said: ". . . the poorest man may in his cottage bid defiance to all the forces of the Crown. It may be frail—its roof may shake—the wind may blow through it—the storms may enter—the rain may enter—but the King of England cannot enter!—all his force dares not cross the threshold of the ruined tenement."

The colonists were familiar with the long struggle in England to secure rights against illegal searches and seizures. A 1591 law authorized magistrates to question anyone they desired and to search all suspected places for papers of a threatening political character. An anti-Catholic law of 1606 authorized searches in the "Howses and Lodgings of every Popishe Recusant" and the destruction of anything judged "unmeete for such Recusant . . . to have or own." The law was later expanded to include political as well as religious dissidents.

The efforts of one of England's most famous jurists, Sir Edward Coke, to win security for home and property were well known in America. In his famous *Institutes,* Coke cited the Magna Carta of 1215 as prohibiting illegal searches. Ironically, when Coke died, King Charles I directed that his house and chambers be ransacked. The manuscript of the *Institutes* was confiscated as "seditious . . . dangerous [and] disadvantageous to His Majesty's service."

John Wilkes, a member of Parliament, dealt a significant blow against illegal searches. Wilkes was arrested on a general warrant (allowing arrest for unstated causes or arrest, search, or seizure of unspecified persons, places, or objects) in 1763 and charged with seditious libel. He was jailed in the infamous Tower of London, and his house was ransacked and his papers searched. Wilkes charged the raiders with illegal trespass. A chief justice found in favor of Wilkes and said that "to enter a man's house by virtue of a nameless warrant . . . is worse than the Spanish inquisition. . . ." After a long struggle, Wilkes was vindicated and returned to Parliament.

Wilkes was a hero to the American colonists, who saw abuses of search and seizure continuing in their communities in the years before the Revolution. Crown authorities raided homes, barns, stores, and warehouses, looking for seditious documents and weapons as well as smuggled goods. Under these "writs of assistance," which were, in effect, general warrants, any suspicious

AMENDMENT IV – THE RIGHT OF THE PEOPLE TO BE SECURE IN THEIR PERSONS, HOUSES, PAPERS, AND EFFECTS, AGAINST UNREASONABLE SEARCHES AND SEIZURES, SHALL NOT BE VIOLATED, AND NO WARRANTS SHALL ISSUE, BUT UPON PROBABLE CAUSE, SUPPORTED BY OATH OR AFFIRMATION, AND PARTICULARLY DESCRIBING THE PLACE TO BE SEARCHED, AND THE PERSONS OR THINGS TO BE SEIZED.

Secure in One's Home *by Dana Verkouteren, 1990 (left).*
A police officer searching a person for weapons
at the scene of an arrest is an example of a reasonable
search not requiring a warrant (right).

35

item found during the searches could be used as evidence, even though the individual involved had not been charged with a crime.

At a 1772 meeting in Boston colonists drafted a document entitled *The Rights of the Colonists and a List of Infringements and Violations of Rights.* The document, circulated throughout the colonies as the *Boston Pamphlet,* listed rights considered fundamental, including some not previously declared in colonial charters. Foremost among these was the right against unreasonable searches and seizures, without which "Officers . . . break thro' the sacred rights of the *Domicil,* ransack men's houses, destroy their securities, carry off their property, and . . . commit the most horred murders."

When the states met in their separate conventions to ratify the new Constitution, over 200 different amendments were proposed to strengthen individual rights, including proposals from five states that formed the core of the Fourth Amendment.

The Fourth Amendment has two parts: the first protects citizens against unreasonable searches and seizures; the second part defines the procedure for issuing a warrant. The Amendment spells out "unreasonable" searches to allow for those occasions of reasonable search when no warrant is required. For example, as courts have interpreted the amendment, a police officer may with certain exceptions search a motor vehicle without a warrant. In most instances where a person is merely suspected of a crime, a warrant to search for evidence is required. A judge or magistrate issues a warrant after police officers have demonstrated that there is "probable cause" to believe that a crime has been committed.

To protect individuals from illegal searches, the Supreme Court has ruled that evidence seized in violation of the Fourth Amendment may not be introduced as evidence in court. This is called the *exclusionary rule* and dates back to 1914 in federal jurisdictions and to 1961 for the states.

Protection against illegal searches and seizures has been fortified over the years by statutes and Supreme Court rulings. In making its decisions, however, the Supreme Court has balanced individual privacy against public security in a changing society. As a result, the laws governing search and seizure have become complex, with sometimes fine distinctions between what is and is not allowed. For example, in a recent decision involving stolen property, the Court ruled that police officers who noticed stolen stereos in an apartment while there to investigate an unrelated crime were not committing an illegal search by merely observing what was in plain view. This decision was in keeping with what has come to be called the "plain view" doctrine.

Technological advances now provide the means to intrude on the privacy of the home that are difficult to detect, such as wiretapping and other forms of electronic eavesdropping. State and federal laws have included these devices under constitutional guarantees against unlawful search and seizure.

Two young people are stopped by a police officer at a sobriety checkpoint (above). Before conducting a search, police must obtain a warrant by convincing a judge of "probable cause" that a crime has been committed (right).

AO 93 (Rev. 5/85) Search Warrant

United States District Court

DISTRICT OF

In the Matter of the Search of
(Name, address or brief description of person or property to be searched)

SEARCH WARRANT

CASE NUMBER:

TO: _____ and any Authorized Officer of the United States

Affidavit(s) having been made before me by _____ who has reason to
believe that ☐ on the person of or ☐ on the premises known as (name, description and/or location)

in the _____ District of _____ there is now
concealed a certain person or property, namely (describe the person or property)

I am satisfied that the affidavit(s) and any recorded testimony establish probable cause to believe that the person
or property so described is now concealed on the person or premises above-described and establish grounds for
the issuance of this warrant.

YOU ARE HEREBY COMMANDED to search on or before _____
                                                          Date
(not to exceed 10 days) the person or place named above for the person or property specified, serving this warrant
and making the search (in the daytime — 6:00 A.M. to 10:00 P.M.) (at any time in the day or night as I find
reasonable cause has been established) and if the person or property be found there to seize same, leaving a copy
of this warrant and receipt for the person or property taken, and prepare a written inventory of the person or property seized and promptly return this warrant to
as required by law.   U.S. Judge or Magistrate

_____   at _____
Date and Time Issued   City and State

_____   _____
Name and Title of Judicial Officer   Signature of Judicial Officer

April 10, 1696 Parliament passes the Navigation Act, giving colonial customs officers wide powers in searching for contraband, including the right to use Writs of Assistance (first authorized by Parliament in 1662).

February 24, 1761 James Otis condemns the British Writs of Assistance as a violation of the English common law principle that a man's house is his castle.

April 5, 1764 Parliament reorganizes the customs system, which establishes a vice-admiralty court in Halifax, Nova Scotia, with wide powers of search and seizure over the American colonies.

1765 British courts rule in *Leach v. Money* and *Entick v. Carrington* that general warrants are illegal.

February 1, 1886 The Supreme Court rules in *Boyd v. United States* that a revenue statute requiring production of private papers is unconstitutional as unreasonable search and seizure.

February 24, 1914 The Supreme Court decides in *Weeks v. United States* that illegally seized evidence must be excluded from federal trials.

June 27, 1949 The Supreme Court decides in *Wolf v. Colorado* that the federal requirement of exclusion of illegally seized evidence is not imposed on the states by the due process clause of the Fourteenth Amendment.

June 19, 1961 The Supreme Court decides in *Mapp v. Ohio* that the federal requirement of exclusion of illegally seized evidence is imposed on the states by the due process clause of the Fourteenth Amendment.

June 19, 1968 Congress passes the Federal Wiretap Act permitting state and federal police to tap telephones provided they receive judicial authorization. In national security cases, the President has been given power to wiretap without prior judicial approval.

The Fifth Amendment

The Fifth Amendment protection against self-incrimination might not have become part of our Constitution had it not been for the American patriot, Alexander McDougall. His 1770 handbill opposing colonial support for and quartering of British troops began "To the Betrayed Inhabitants of New-York." For publishing it the state charged McDougall with "false, seditious, and infamous libel." McDougall refused to post bail and remained in jail for 11 weeks while his case became a sensation throughout the colonies. The grand jury, handpicked by the government, indicted McDougall on the libel charge, but the case was dismissed when the state's sole witness died.

The New York Assembly then attempted to convict McDougall by circumventing the courts and issuing a Bill of Attainder for McDougall to be tried before the entire assembly, a practice the United States Constitution would later explicitly prohibit. Hoping to force him into self-incrimination because it had no other basis for holding him, the assembly pressed McDougall to submit written objections to the charge. McDougall's inflammatory response provided the assembly with the libel finding it sought. The assembly found him guilty and he was jailed. When a local judge tried to free McDougall with a writ of *habeas corpus*, the sheriff refused to release him from prison until the assembly adjourned for the year. The incident did not deter McDougall from expressing his free-spirited views. He went on to serve with distinction in the Continental Army and rose to the rank of major general.

ALEXANDER MCDOUGALL
1732-1786

AMENDMENT V – NO PERSON SHALL BE HELD TO ANSWER FOR A CAPITAL, OR OTHERWISE INFAMOUS CRIME, UNLESS ON A PRESENTMENT OR INDICTMENT OF A GRAND JURY, EXCEPT IN CASES ARISING IN THE LAND OR NAVAL FORCES, OR IN THE MILITIA, WHEN IN ACTUAL SERVICE IN TIME OF WAR OR PUBLIC DANGER; NOR SHALL ANY PERSON BE SUBJECT FOR THE SAME OFFENSE TO BE TWICE PUT IN JEOPARDY OF LIFE OR LIMB, NOR SHALL BE COMPELLED IN ANY CRIMINAL CASE TO BE A WITNESS AGAINST HIMSELF, NOR BE DEPRIVED OF LIFE, LIBERTY, OR PROPERTY, WITHOUT DUE PROCESS OF LAW; NOR SHALL PRIVATE PROPERTY BE TAKEN FOR PUBLIC USE WITHOUT JUST COMPENSATION.

*T*he Fifth Amendment protects an individual's "life, liberty, and property" by specifying certain procedures that the government must follow in the legal system. It includes protection in cases of criminal prosecution and in the appropriation of private property for public use.

Perhaps the best-known provision of the Fifth Amendment is the clause against forced "self-incrimination," whose origin goes back to the days when persons accused of crimes before English ecclesiastical courts were forced to take an *ex officio* oath. That is, they had to swear to answer all questions even if the questions did not apply to the case at trial. This requirement was later adopted by the Court of Star Chamber.

One of the victims of the Court was a printer and book distributor named John Lilburne, charged in 1637 with treason for importing books "that promoted Puritan dissent." Lilburne told his accusers, "I am not willing to answer you to any more of these questions because I see you go about by this examination to ensnare me. For seeing the things for which I am imprisoned cannot be proved against me, you will get other material out of my examination; and therefore if you will not ask me about the thing laid to my charge, I shall answer no more. . . . I think by the law of the land, that I may stand upon my just defense."

Lilburne was convicted, fined, whipped, pilloried, gagged, and imprisoned until he agreed to take the oath. The brutality of his treatment helped bring about the end of Star Chamber. Later he published *An Agreement of the Free People of England,* one of the first proposals ever made for a written constitution. It included a guarantee against forced self-incrimination and of other provisions that eventually found their way into the American Bill of Rights.

One notorious instance of forced self-incrimination in the American colonies occurred in the Salem witch trials. In 1692 Giles Corey, an elderly Massachusetts farmer, was accused of witchcraft. Wishing to assure that his heirs inherited his property, he refused to plead. He knew that whether he pleaded guilty or not guilty, he would have been convicted and executed and his property confiscated. If he refused to plead, he could not be convicted. The judges ordered him strapped to a table, and stones were loaded upon his chest to force a plea out of him. Corey's final words were "more weight." Then his chest caved in.

At the time of the drafting of the Constitution in 1787, only six of the 13 states had provisions against compelled self-incrimination in their constitutions. When the Constitution was sent to the states for ratification, only four states suggested an amendment against self-incrimination.

Although the right to "take the Fifth" to avoid forced self-incrimination is familiar to most Americans through televised

The [Salem witch] Trial of George Jacobs, August 5, 1692, *by T. H. Matteson, 1833, (upper left). "Taking the Fifth," an expression popularized during hearings on organized crime led by Senator Estes Kefauver, standing (above). Suspects in custody must be informed of their rights before any interrogation begins (right).*

WARNING AS TO YOUR RIGHTS

You are under arrest. Before we ask you any questions, you must understand what your rights are.

You have the right to remain silent. You are not required to say anything to us at any time or to answer any questions. Anything you say can be used against you in court.

You have the right to talk to a lawyer for advice before we question you and to have him with you during questioning.

If you cannot afford a lawyer and want one, a lawyer will be provided for you.

If you want to answer questions now without a lawyer present you will still have the right to stop answering at any time. You also have the right to stop answering at any time until you talk to a lawyer.

DO YOU UNDERSTAND YOUR RIGHTS?

2020-164

February 13, 1645 The English House of Lords sets aside conviction of Puritan publisher, John Lilburne, on grounds of forced self-incrimination.

September 1, 1807 Aaron Burr is acquitted of charge of treason in trial in Richmond, Virginia.

July 2, 1861 President Lincoln authorizes suspension of right of *habeas corpus* in certain cases.

March 3, 1884 The Supreme Court rules in *Hurtado v. California* that the Fourteenth Amendment does not require a grand jury procedure in the states.

February 19, 1942 President Roosevelt authorizes removal of Japanese and Japanese-Americans to internment camps.

February 7, 1950 Senator Joseph McCarthy of Wisconsin charges the State Department with harboring Communists; charges lead to a series of Congressional investigations.

March 12, 1951 The "Kefauver Hearings" into organized crime begin; TV coverage makes "taking the Fifth" familiar to the public.

April 9, 1956 The Supreme Court in *Slochower v. Board of Education of New York* declares unconstitutional the discharge of public employees for invoking the guarantee against forced self-incrimination.

June 15, 1964 The Supreme Court in *Malloy v. Hogan* applies protections of self-incrimination clause to states through the Fourteenth Amendment.

June 13, 1966 The Supreme Court in *Miranda v. Arizona* rules that a suspect must be informed of his legal rights before custodial interrogations, to ensure that confessions are voluntary, not coerced.

Congressional hearings, the right also protects citizens — guilty and innocent alike — from the power of the police and the courts. "Taking the Fifth" reinforces the idea that one is innocent until proved guilty, and it means that the prosecution must find evidence other than testimony forced from the accused. Today a witness in any governmental proceeding may refuse to answer any question if the answer might be used against him or her in a future criminal proceeding. As the Supreme Court has said, "A witness may have a reasonable fear of prosecution and yet be innocent of any wrongdoing."

To the charge that the Fifth Amendment is only a shield for the guilty, Justice William O. Douglas answered, "Those who would attach a sinister meaning to the invocation of the Fifth Amendment have forgotten . . . history. For, from the beginning, the dignity of man cried out against compulsion. If the individual's spirit of liberty is to be kept alive, if government is to be civilized in its relation to the citizen, no form of compulsion should be used to exact evidence from him that might convict him."

The Amendment specifies that an individual cannot be charged by the federal government with a capital or other serious crime unless a "Grand Jury" of fellow citizens has found sufficient evidence to warrant an indictment. Government is thus prevented from harassing citizens with serious but unfounded charges.

The "double jeopardy" provision in the Fifth Amendment means that a person cannot be tried twice for the same offense in the same jurisdiction, once a verdict of acquittal has been made. The individual may, however, be tried a second time in another jurisdiction if a jury cannot agree on a verdict, a mistrial is declared for some other reason, or he or she requests a new trial.

The "takings clause" of the Fifth Amendment assures that when private property is taken by the government for public use (i.e., through the power of eminent domain), the owners will be justly compensated.

Perhaps the most important phrase in the Fifth Amendment is the guarantee of no deprivation of "life, liberty, and property" without "due process of law." This expresses a principle at least as old as the Magna Carta of 1215, which prohibited the king from imprisoning or harming a person "except by the lawful judgment of his peers or by the law of the land." A 1354 Act of Parliament reconfirming the Magna Carta paraphrased its Article 39 and changed "by law of the land" to "due process of law."

The phrase "due process of law" is in many ways the parent of all the procedural rights guaranteed by the Constitution. Over the years courts have repeatedly been called upon to interpret the meaning of due process, both in the Fifth and Fourteenth Amendments. Today "due process of law" is one of the most important and influential terms in American constitutional law.

The Sixth, Seventh and Eighth Amendments

The guarantees of the Sixth, Seventh, and Eighth Amendments were added to the Constitution in part because of a famous English trial over a hundred years earlier. The government of Charles II had forbidden William Penn, a Quaker, to speak in public. Penn ignored the prohibition and was promptly arrested for riot and tumultuous assembly.

At the trial, the judge, noting that Penn had removed his hat, arbitrarily ordered him to put it back on — and then immediately charged him with contempt for wearing a hat in court. The court then ordered Penn removed for the duration of the trial, a gross violation of English common law. As he was led away, Penn cried out, "I appeal to the jurors who are my judges . . . whether the proceedings of the court are not most arbitrary and void of all law."

After testimony about Penn's public speaking, the court ordered a verdict of "Guilty of Unlawful Assembly." But the jury found Penn guilty only of "speaking in Gracechurch Street" and "allowed no such word as an unlawful assembly in their verdict." Such defiance outraged the judge, who ordered the jury jailed indefinitely without food or water. This abuse of the jury was a common court practice to assure an acceptable verdict. The jury remained adamant, however, and the frustrated judge finally gave in and accepted the decision. The judge got his revenge, though, by jailing Penn until he paid a substantial fine for wearing his hat "in the face of authority."

WILLIAM PENN
1644-1718

AMENDMENT VI – IN ALL CRIMINAL PROSECUTIONS, THE ACCUSED SHALL ENJOY THE RIGHT TO A SPEEDY AND PUBLIC TRIAL, BY AN IMPARTIAL JURY OF THE STATE AND DISTRICT WHEREIN THE CRIME SHALL HAVE BEEN COMMITTED; WHICH DISTRICT SHALL HAVE BEEN PREVIOUSLY ASCERTAINED BY LAW, AND TO BE INFORMED OF THE NATURE AND CAUSES OF THE ACCUSATION; TO BE CONFRONTED WITH THE WITNESSES AGAINST HIM; TO HAVE COMPULSORY PROCESS FOR OBTAINING WITNESSES IN HIS FAVOR, AND TO HAVE THE ASSISTANCE OF COUNSEL FOR HIS DEFENCE.

AMENDMENT VII – IN SUITS AT COMMON LAW, WHERE THE VALUE IN CONTROVERSY SHALL EXCEED TWENTY DOLLARS, THE RIGHT OF TRIAL BY JURY SHALL BE PRESERVED, AND NO FACT TRIED BY A JURY SHALL BE OTHERWISE RE-EXAMINED IN ANY COURT OF THE UNITED STATES, THAN ACCORDING TO THE RULES OF THE COMMON LAW.

AMENDMENT VIII – EXCESSIVE BAIL SHALL NOT BE REQUIRED, NOR EXCESSIVE FINES IMPOSED, NOR CRUEL AND UNUSUAL PUNISHMENTS INFLICTED.

The Jury *by Phillip Rattner (1964).*

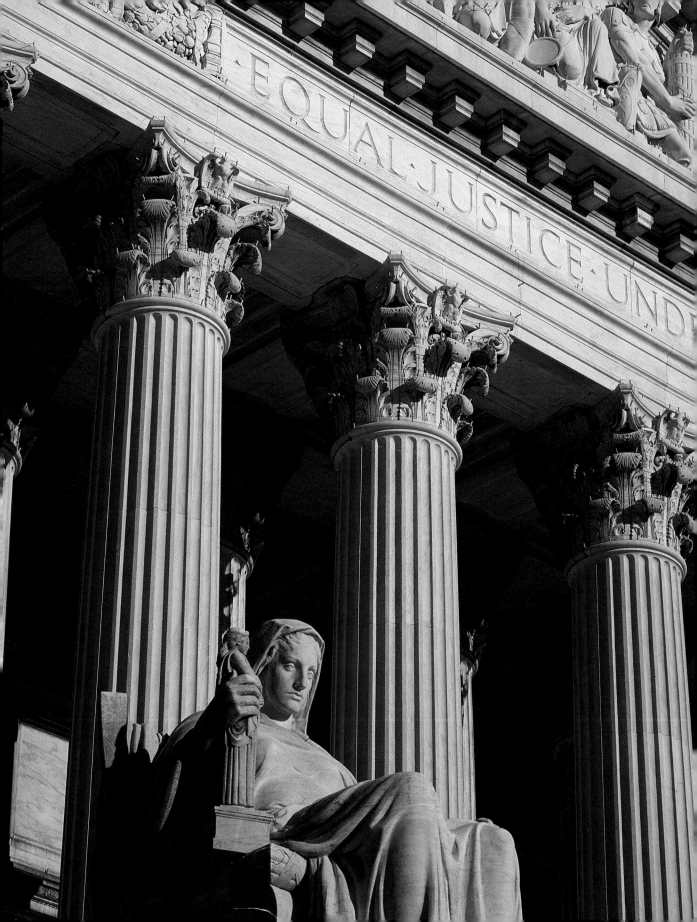

*S*everal amendments in the Bill of Rights lay down the rules government must follow when it takes action against or decides disputes between citizens. The Sixth through Eighth Amendments fall into this category. They have to do with basic protections against arbitrary government.

In many respects, the Framers of the Constitution considered these rights the most important. Experience had shown that in government's administration of the law lay the greatest potential for tyranny. This is perhaps why most of the fundamental rights written into the original Constitution before the Bill of Rights — including trial by jury and writ of *habeas corpus* — address judicial procedures. Together with the provisions of the Fourth and Fifth Amendments, the Sixth through Eighth Amendments went further in spelling out the fundamentals of "due process" in the government's enforcement of the law. They not only secured the right of trial by jury but also included those guarantees meant to assure a fair trial and, for those duly convicted, appropriate punishment as well.

The origins of the jury system are found in the law of medieval England. For centuries a variety of customary procedures had existed to determine the guilt or innocence of an accused person, including trial by combat and trial by ordeal. In one application of the latter, the accused party was made to walk a few paces while holding a red-hot iron. If the resulting burns healed after three days, the defendant was found innocent; if not, guilty.

Gradually the jury system evolved with the development of the royal courts of England. Adapted from the French inquest procedure, the system was originally a device whereby "twelve men tried and true" were summoned by the court to provide evidence in a particular case. Eventually, its role changed from the giving to the weighing of evidence, but from the beginning the institution of the jury provided the commonsense judgment of the community and served as a bulwark against arbitrary power.

Trial by ordeal was abolished in 1219, four years after the Magna Carta. Article 39 of the Great Charter, which speaks about "lawful judgment of peers" and the "law of the land," was at one time

"Equal Justice Under Law," the legend over
the portico of the Supreme Court of the United States.

47

interpreted as guaranteeing trial by jury. Actually, as a feudal document protecting the privileges of barons and clergy, the Great Charter did no such thing. But Centuries later, long after feudalism itself had disappeared, the Magna Carta did take on a greater historical importance in its broad articulation of the principle of due process, including the right to a speedy trial according to the law of the land.

In the 17th century Sir Edward Coke and other champions of English liberty invoked the Great Charter against the high-handed actions of the Stuart kings. Royal abuses of the Court of Star Chamber, including imprisonment without cause and denial of bail, struck at what we consider the very fundamentals of justice. The successful struggle on behalf of these fundamentals had a profound impact upon American as well as English thinking. The English Bill of Rights of 1689, one of the key texts for our own Bill of Rights, provided guarantees for trial by jury, and prohibited excessive bails and fines, as well as "cruel and unusual punishment."

From the earliest settlements, American colonists had practiced trial by jury. Many of the colonial charters proclaimed this and other judicial guarantees. Although the British government appointed royal judges to the colonies, their salaries were provided by local legislatures and, in most instances, these judges were familiar with the communities for which they were responsible. This local autonomy in the administration of law came under attack in the events leading up to the American Revolution. Colonial resistance to British authority led the government in London to curtail much of this judicial autonomy. The government made colonial judges subservient to the crown and decreed that for certain crimes colonists could be taken to Britain for trial. Such measures meant both justice delayed and justice denied, in prolonged imprisonment before trial and in the denial of supporting witnesses and a proper jury. The deep-seated resentment of such measures found expression in the Declaration of Independence.

The Framers recognized the supreme importance of the right to trial by jury by including it in the Constitution. Many who opposed the Constitution's ratification, however, believed that the simple guarantee of trial by jury in criminal cases was insufficient. They wanted additional guarantees spelled out much as they had been in the Northwest Ordinance of 1787. In the end, there was little disagreement in the passage of the Bill of Rights about the several specifics of due process articulated in the Sixth Amendment.

There had been disagreement, however, over whether or not the guarantee of trial by jury should be extended to civil cases. Those opposed pointed out that the diversity in civil law made such a guarantee impractical. James Iredell, who later became one of the first Associate Justices of the Supreme Court, explained to George Mason that civil cases had not been included because it was a

> *"To no one will we sell, to no one will we refuse or delay, right or justice."*
> MAGNA CARTA
> 1215

> *"He [King George III] has . . . depriv[ed] us, in many Cases, of the Benefits of Trial by Jury . . . transporting us beyond Seas to be tried for pretended offences. . . ."*
> DECLARATION
> OF INDEPENDENCE
> 1776

"complicated business," better left to "future legislatures." Mason believed otherwise. Hadn't such a guarantee been included in the Virginia Declaration of Rights? There Mason had written, "In controversies respecting property, and in suits between man and man, the ancient trial by jury is one of the greatest securities to the rights of the people, and to remain sacred and inviolable."

In the end, the Seventh Amendment included in the Bill of Rights a provision for trial by jury in civil cases. It assured that the federal government would honor the status quo of the jury system in civil law cases, and that is how the courts have generally read the amendment ever since.

Uncertainty about what the Framers of the Constitution meant by the phrase "cruel and unusual punishment" has made interpretation of the Eighth Amendment difficult. In general, the amendment has been taken to mean punishment that is either inappropriate in itself (for example, torture) or that is grossly disproportionate to the crime for which it is being applied.

Because the courts have usually deferred to current community values, especially as expressed through the legislative branch of government, in interpreting "cruel and unusual punishment," opponents of the death penalty and of corporal punishment have generally been unsuccessful in invoking the Eighth Amendment. The courts have applied the amendment, however, to strike down laws where the punishment does not fit the crime and to improve prison conditions.

The Fourteenth Amendment dramatically enlarged the potential application of these judicial guarantees when, in 1868, it extended the requirements of due process to the states. Perhaps the most significant changes in recent decades have had to do with the Sixth Amendment guarantee of the right to counsel. In its 1963 decision in *Gideon v. Wainwright,* the Supreme Court ruled that a state had to provide counsel for indigents accused of a serious crime. In a subsequent decision, based on the Fifth Amendment, the Court ruled in *Miranda v. Arizona* (1966) that the right to counsel extended to suspects in custody as well.

In recent decades the nation's courts have confronted a number of constitutional issues arising from the Sixth through Eighth Amendments. For example, is television and radio coverage of courtroom proceedings consistent with the right to a fair trial? Is videotaped testimony consistent with the right to confront one's accusers? Is a nonunanimous verdict or a verdict by a jury of less than 12 members consistent with constitutional requirements?

By adapting ancient principles and institutions such as the jury system to the changing circumstances of the modern world, the Constitution has secured the most fundamental and surest guarantee of our freedom: equal justice under law.

The pillory was a punishment device that caused pain and exposed the offenders to public scorn.

RURAL LIFE MUSEUM, LOUISIANA STATE UNIVERSITY, PHOTO: PRATHER WARREN

November 9, 1670 A jury defies the king's judge and finds William Penn not guilty of a breach of the peace; this action represents a triumph of the jury system.

November 7, 1932 The Supreme Court orders a new trial for the "Scottsboro boys," charged with the capital crime of rape, on the basis of the Sixth Amendment guarantee of the right to counsel.

November 23, 1953 President Eisenhower, in reference to the tactics of Senator McCarthy, says that Americans have the right to confront their accusers face to face.

March 18, 1963 The Supreme Court provides in *Gideon v. Wainwright* new safeguards in the Sixth Amendment guarantee of the right to counsel.

June 29, 1972 The Supreme Court declares in *Furman v. Georgia* that current application of capital punishment by the states violates the Eighth Amendment.

July 2, 1976 The Supreme Court rules in *Gregg v. Georgia* that the death penalty as punishment for first-degree murder is not inherently in violation of the Constitution.

April 19, 1977 The Supreme Court rules in *Ingraham v. Wright* that use of corporal punishment by schools does not violate the Eighth Amendment.

The Ninth and Tenth Amendments

The Ninth and Tenth Amendments were adopted in part to satisfy Anti-Federalist fears of a strong national government. More than any other constitutional provision, they raise the question of the nature of the Federal Union, the centerpiece of constitutional debate preceding the Civil War. As the young republic wrestled for decades with conflicting sectional interests, the debate produced very different views of the Union, articulated by two senatorial giants of that era.

John C. Calhoun of South Carolina resigned the Vice Presidency in 1832 to champion the cause of states' rights in the Senate. He argued his principle of nullification, which held that a state retained with its original sovereignty the authority to overrule federal actions that it considered unconstitutional. For Calhoun the Constitution was a contract representing a "government of States united in political union." Calhoun saw in the doctrine of nullification and, if necessary, secession, the fundamental guarantee of liberty that, more than the Union itself, he held most dear.

Calhoun was countered by the dynamic Daniel Webster of New Hampshire, who denied that ultimate sovereignty rested with the states. Instead, the Constitution embodied the sovereignty of the American people as a whole in a transcendent and perpetual union. Maintaining that it was "the people's Constitution, . . . made by the people," Webster declared, "Liberty and Union, now and forever, one and inseparable."

Born in the same year, neither Calhoun nor Webster lived to see the resolution of this conflict in the Civil War that both hoped to avoid.

JOHN C. CALHOUN
1782-1850

DANIEL WEBSTER
1782-1852

*T*he first eight amendments in the Bill of Rights contain specific prohibitions on the manner in which the federal government may exercise its powers. Thus, Congress, whatever the military necessity, may not require the peacetime quartering of troops in private homes; nor may it make any religion the official sect. Unlike the specific restraints of Amendments One through Eight, the Ninth and Tenth Amendments hint that there may be limits on the government's power beyond those already specified.

The Ninth Amendment recognizes the personal rights that may be entitled to constitutional protection from government interference. The Tenth, in part a response to Anti-Federalist concerns about the eclipse of state powers upon the adoption of the Constitution, also acknowledges the basic political principle that all powers belong to the people. Only those powers delegated by the

AMENDMENT IX – THE ENUMERATION IN THE CONSTITUTION OF CERTAIN RIGHTS SHALL NOT BE CONSTRUED TO DENY OR DISPARAGE OTHERS RETAINED BY THE PEOPLE.

AMENDMENT X– THE POWERS NOT DELEGATED TO THE UNITED STATES BY THE CONSTITUTION, NOR PROHIBITED BY IT TO THE STATES, ARE RESERVED TO THE STATES RESPECTIVELY, OR TO THE PEOPLE.

Flags of the 50 states displayed in a U.S. Army ceremony to commemorate the National Guard and its role in state and national security (above). Federal funds help states to meet needs of school children (right).

LEE T. ANDERSON

people may be exercised by the government — either federal or state. Thus the Bill of Rights ends on the note sounded at the Constitution's beginning — affirming the sovereign power of "We, the People."

Taken together, these amendments are a curious compromise between the arguments of the Anti-Federalists and Federalists concerning the need for a bill of rights. Federalists, with Alexander Hamilton, argued that the protection of rights depended ultimately "on the general spirit of the people and of the government," and that the Constitution itself was therefore "in every rational sense, and to every useful purpose, a Bill of Rights."

Anti-Federalists, more distrustful of the government, wished to see it limited as strictly as possible. To reinforce these limits, Anti-Federalist Congressmen wanted the Tenth Amendment to limit

PAT LANZA/FOLIO, INC.

"You have rights antecedent to all earthly governments, rights that cannot be repealed or restrained by human law; rights derived from the Great Legislator of the Universe."
JOHN ADAMS

"The proposed Constitution . . . is, in strictness, neither a national nor a federal Constitution, but a composition of both . . . it is partly federal and partly national."
JAMES MADISON
Federalist No. 39

Congress to the powers "expressly delegated"—the language of the Articles of Confederation. In debate, James Madison pointed out that "it was impossible to confine a government to the exercise of *express* powers; there must necessarily be admitted powers by implication. . . ."

If the federal government were acknowledged to possess "implied" powers by direct grant of the people, Anti-Federalists feared, it might be impossible for the states to resist extensions of federal power over them. At issue was the very nature of the Union created by the Constitution. Was it created by "the People," acting as the sovereign power, or was it created by the states, which agreed to give up certain powers to the central government?

Twice, in the Kentucky and Virginia Resolutions of 1798 and again in South Carolina's Ordinance of Nullification in 1832, states attempted to assert their sovereign power to declare Acts of Congress to be exercises of powers not delegated and thus unconstitutional. The Virginia Resolutions were drafted by James Madison; they reversed, at least temporarily, his earlier views and took a "states' rights" position. Although both attempts were unsuccessful, they kept alive the theory that the Constitution was a "compact," or contract, among sovereign states. This theory was the foundation of the doctrine, acted out by the southern states in 1860, that a state could secede from the Union.

It took the cataclysm of the Civil War to settle the issue of the primacy of the federal government through domestic affairs. Following the war, the federal government, by Acts of Congress, executive actions, and Supreme Court decisions, expanded its authority and influence within the states. This power was manifested in the role of the federal government during Reconstruction, the New Deal, and more recently in civil rights enforcement. In recent years, courts and successive administrations have sought a realignment of federal and state responsibilities, under such rubrics as "creative federalism" or "new federalism." Such initiatives demonstrate that the idea of divided powers expressed in the Tenth Amendment still influences our system of government.

Despite their profound theoretical significance for the nature of our government, few if any court cases have ever been decided on Ninth or Tenth Amendment grounds, although minorities on the Court have suggested that they are prepared to do so. Thus no rights have been identified as rights protected by the Ninth Amendment, and so far no court has found a power claimed by the federal government that is "reserved to the States . . . or to the people."

Perhaps one reason for this is that these amendments are vague enough to support many interpretations. The Tenth Amendment, for example, could be made compatible with either the sovereign people of the James Madison of 1787, or the sovereign states of the James Madison of 1798, or with John C. Calhoun. As for the rights protected by the Ninth Amendment, there may come a day when a majority of the Supreme Court will begin to identify them, as the late Justice Arthur Goldberg and others urged.

Civil War reenactments recall the price of unity (above). Federal and state funds are pooled to build highways (left).

July 10, 1754 Delegates to the Albany Congress approve Benjamin Franklin's "Plan of Union," providing for a federation of most of the American colonies under a president general.

April/May 1776 The Continental Congress informs former British colonies that they might begin to write constitutions of their own in order to become states.

Nov./Dec. 1798 The Kentucky and Virginia Resolutions articulate a state's right to protest policies of the federal government.

December 1814 Delegates from New England states, upset with the policies of the Madison Administration, meet in the Hartford Convention to begin talk of secession.

December 19, 1828 South Carolina legislature orders publication of John C. Calhoun's doctrine of nullification.

January 12–27, 1830 The Webster-Hayne debates over nature of the Union and states' rights take place.

November 24, 1832 South Carolina seeks to nullify the Tariff Acts of 1828 and 1832.

December 20, 1860 South Carolina becomes the first state to secede from the Union in the prelude to the Civil War.

March 2, 1867 Congress passes the First Reconstruction Act, establishing military government in the former Confederate states and criteria for restoring their legitimacy in the Union.

June 7, 1965 Supreme Court Justice Arthur Goldberg cites the right of privacy under the Ninth Amendment in a separate opinion in *Griswold v. Connecticut.*

October 13, 1969 President Richard Nixon's "New Federalism" program, calling for a broad range of reforms in federal and state governments, is presented to Congress.

The Thirteenth, Fourteenth and Fifteenth Amendments

One night in 1841, at a meeting of the predominantly white Anti-Slavery Society, an escaped slave in attendance spoke impromptu about his experiences in bondage. The young man so impressed the audience with his intellect and oratory that William Lloyd Garrison, the prominent abolitionist, hired him to speak throughout the country for the abolition of slavery. The young man was Frederick Bailey, who later changed his surname to Douglass to throw the bounty hunters off his trail. As Douglass traveled, his fame spread, but his worries about being forced back into slavery increased. He fled to England until he was able to pay the price for his legal freedom.

Back in the United States, Douglass did not limit his activities to the abolitionist struggle. He wrote in his newspaper, *North Star,* "I am for any movement whenever and wherever there is a good cause to promote, right to assert . . . or a wrong to be redressed."

Douglass went on to play a prominent role in the Civil War. A close friend of Abraham Lincoln, he convinced the President to recruit black regiments and to pay and rank them equally with other Union troops. After the war, he served in several government positions that culminated in his appointment as ambassador to Haiti in 1889.

FREDERICK DOUGLASS
1817-1895

AMENDMENT XIII — SECTION 1. NEITHER SLAVERY NOR INVOLUNTARY SERVITUDE, EXCEPT AS A PUNISHMENT FOR CRIME WHEREOF THE PARTY SHALL HAVE BEEN DULY CONVICTED, SHALL EXIST WITHIN THE UNITED STATES, OR ANY PLACE SUBJECT TO THEIR JURISDICTION.

AMENDMENT XIV — SECTION 2. . . . BUT WHEN THE RIGHT TO VOTE AT ANY ELECTION . . . IS DENIED TO ANY OF THE MALE INHABITANTS OF SUCH STATE . . . THE BASIS OF REPRESENTATION THEREIN SHALL BE REDUCED . . .

SECTION 3. NO PERSON SHALL . . . HOLD ANY OFFICE . . . UNDER THE UNITED STATES, OR UNDER ANY STATE, WHO, HAVING PREVIOUSLY TAKEN AN OATH . . . TO SUPPORT THE CONSTITUTION OF THE UNITED STATES, SHALL HAVE ENGAGED IN INSURRECTION OR REBELLION AGAINST THE SAME . . .

SECTION 4. . . . NEITHER THE UNITED STATES NOR ANY STATE SHALL ASSUME OR PAY ANY DEBT OR OBLIGATION INCURRED IN AID OF INSURRECTION . . . AGAINST THE UNITED STATES, OR ANY CLAIM FOR THE LOSS OF EMANCIPATION OR ANY SLAVE . . .

AMENDMENT XV — SECTION 1. THE RIGHT OF CITIZENS OF THE UNITED STATES TO VOTE SHALL NOT BE DENIED OR ABRIDGED BY THE UNITED STATES OR BY ANY STATE ON ACCOUNT OF RACE, COLOR, OR PREVIOUS CONDITION OF SERVITUDE.

The Shaw Memorial by Augustus Saint-Gaudens — a statue on the Boston Commons commemorating the black soldiers who served in the Civil War (above). The Underground Railroad by Charles T. Webber, 1893 (right).

59

Pennsylvania and Virginia Regimental Civil War flags (above). Abolitionists adopted the Liberty Bell as their symbol. The bell's inscription reads, "Proclaim Liberty Throughout All The Land Unto All The Inhabitants Thereof" (right).

$\mathcal{T}$he Thirteenth, Fourteenth, and Fifteenth Amendments, called the "Civil War Amendments," were designed not only to abolish slavery but also to allow former slaves to participate as citizens in a country in which "liberty and justice for all" had been denied. The Framers of the Constitution were unable to resolve the question of slavery, which figured prominently in the ratification debates. One step toward eradication was taken when the Northwest Ordinance banned slavery in much of the western territories. The Constitution itself declared that the slave trade could end in 1808 or thereafter. And, indeed, Congress passed a law ending the slave trade on the earliest possible date.

The institution of slavery, however, remained. By 1790 there were half a million slaves in the country, and on the eve of the Civil War, the black population in America had risen to 4,500,000, of whom more than 4,000,000 were slaves. By the 1840s the balance in the U.S. Senate between representatives of slave and free states—created by the Missouri Compromise of 1820—became the focus of southern strategy. Southern states wanted to deny Congress the power to interfere with slavery in the federal territories; northern states wanted to limit the expansion of slavery. In 1854 the Kansas-Nebraska Act gave settlers in these territories the right to decide for themselves whether the new states would be slave or free.

The Supreme Court eventually became involved in the issue. On March 6, 1857, Chief Justice Roger Taney, a Maryland tobacco plantation heir who had earlier freed his own slaves, ruled that Dred Scott, a slave who had sued for his freedom on the grounds that he had lived in a free state, "is not a citizen . . . and is not, therefore, entitled to sue in the United States courts." Taney also declared the Missouri Compromise unconstitutional because Congress could not deprive a citizen of his property without due process of the law as guaranteed in the Fifth Amendment. He added that since a slave was property, slavery could not be banned in the territories.

In the end, the issue was not decided in a court of law but by test of convictions and force of arms. Americans had never been at ease with slavery. Anti-slavery societies had been active since the American Revolution. The American Anti-Slavery Society was founded in 1833 and its membership grew to 250,000 in 15 states by 1840. Appealing to both the political ideals of the Revolution and the moral injunctions of the Bible, the abolitionists included among their ranks articulate advocates and organizers such as William Lloyd Garrison, Timothy Dwight Weld, Frederick Douglass, and Sojourner Truth, the last two former slaves. Douglass, together with other journalists like John Russwurm and Samuel Cornish, gave voice in their newspapers to the free black community of the North. The abolitionists adopted as their symbol the Old State House Bell in Philadelphia with its motto, "Proclaim liberty throughout all the land unto all the inhabitants thereof," and re-christened it the "Liberty Bell."

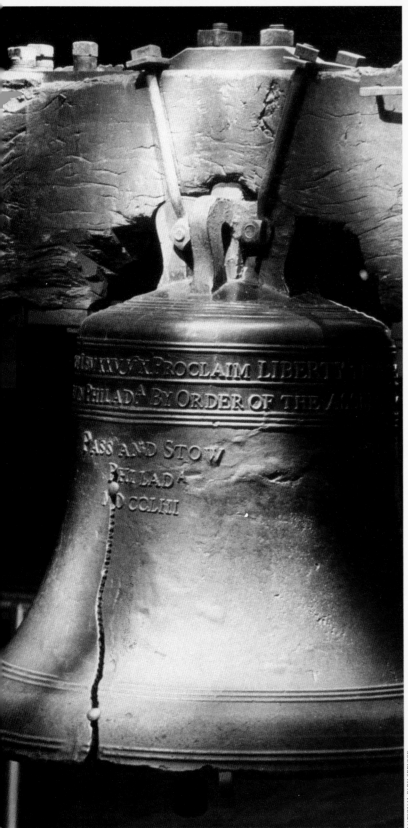

*"That this nation,
under God, shall have a
new birth of freedom. . . ."*
ABRAHAM LINCOLN

*"Though slavery was
abolished, the wrongs of
my people were not ended.
Though they were not
slaves, they were not yet
quite free."*
FREDERICK DOUGLASS

May 18, 1652 Rhode Island enacts the first American law making slavery illegal.

April 14, 1775 First abolition society in America is founded in Philadelphia by Benjamin Franklin and Dr. Benjamin Rush.

March 2, 1807 Congress enacts legislation prohibiting importation of any more slaves after January 1, 1808.

March 3, 1820 The Missouri Compromise, providing for parity in the number of slave and non-slave states and banning slavery in the new territory north of 36° 30′ (other than Missouri), goes into effect.

January 6, 1832 The New England Anti-Slavery Society is formed, aided by William Lloyd Garrison's weekly newspaper, *The Liberator*.

1849 Harriet "Moses" Tubman, soon to be a "conductor" on the "underground railroad," escapes from slavery. Tubman later returns to the South many times to help transport slaves to freedom.

September 9–12, 1850 Congress adopts the five provisions of the Compromise of 1850, appeasing both the pro- and anti-slavery interests. The settlement includes a new Fugitive Slave Act, passed on January 1, 1851.

May 26, 1854 The Kansas-Nebraska Act is passed, allowing "popular sovereignty" to determine the status of slavery in the prospective new states.

March 6, 1857 The Supreme Court delivers the "Dred Scott" decision (*Scott v. Sandford*), overturning the Missouri Compromise and thereby removing limitations on the expansion of slavery.

August 21, 1858 The Lincoln-Douglas debates begin, highlighting the future of slavery as a national issue.

October 16–18, 1859 John Brown and his followers raid Harper's Ferry.

September 22, 1862 President Lincoln issues the Emancipation Proclamation, which goes into effect January 1, 1863.

November 19, 1863 Lincoln delivers the Gettysburg Address.

March 3, 1865 The Freedmen's Bureau, a federal agency to help recently emancipated slaves, is created.

December 6, 1865 The Thirteenth Amendment, abolishing slavery, is ratified (announced officially on December 18, 1865).

July 9, 1868 The Fourteenth Amendment is ratified (announced officially on July 28, 1868).

February 3, 1870 The Fifteenth Amendment, guaranteeing former slaves the right to vote, is ratified (announced officially on March 30, 1870).

February 25, 1870 Hiram R. Revels takes his seat as the first black in the U.S. Senate (R-Mississippi).

April 24, 1877 Reconstruction ends with the withdrawal of the last of the federal forces still policing the South.

The demands of the abolitionists often led to violent confrontations, even with those who opposed slavery, but rejected the methods of the abolitionists. In 1859 the abolitionist zealot John Brown led a raid on the federal arsenal at Harper's Ferry, Virginia; he hoped to arm slaves and incite a slave rebellion. He was captured, tried, and hanged. The Underground Railroad was less violent and more successful in its efforts to free slaves. Maryland native Harriet Tubman became the most famous "conductor" on the Underground Railroad by making 19 trips into the South to free more than 300 slaves.

When Abraham Lincoln was elected in 1860, the South seceded, and the Civil War began. In 1863 Lincoln issued the Emancipation Proclamation, freeing slaves "within any state or designated part of a state" still in rebellion. A year later, in 1864, Congress passed the Thirteenth Amendment, which declared that "neither slavery nor involuntary servitude . . . shall exist within the United States. . . ."

Freeing the slaves was one thing; recognizing their equality and incorporating them into the fabric of national life was another. Even the abolitionist leaders could not decide whether the Thirteenth Amendment was a beginning or an end. Abolitionist William Lloyd Garrison was optimistic. He urged that the American Anti-Slavery Society be dissolved. Frederick Douglass, an eloquent spokesman for black freedom, was less optimistic. He predicted battles to come when he said, "Slavery is not abolished until the black man has the ballot." Although Congress passed a Civil Rights Act in 1866, doubts about its constitutionality convinced Congress that another amendment was necessary. This led to the Fourteenth Amendment.

Sections 2, 3, and 4 of the Fourteenth Amendment, providing the conditions for the South's return to the nation's political life, have passed into history. Section 1, guaranteeing the rights of citizenship and equal protection of the laws to all Americans, continues to hold center stage.

Neither the Thirteenth nor Fourteenth Amendment directly addressed the issue of voting rights that Frederick Douglass foresaw as critical. The Fifteenth Amendment, ratified in 1870, declared that "the right to vote shall not be denied or abridged . . . on account of race, color, or previous condition of servitude." Since the amendment did not mention sex, women regarded their demands as unfulfilled and began to pursue their own agenda.

Attempts to limit the impact of the Fifteenth Amendment became rampant in both the North and the South. Rhode Island required foreign-born citizens to be property owners in order to vote. Massachusetts instituted a literacy test, and California simply excluded Chinese from voter rolls. In the South voter discrimination included "grandfather clauses," literacy tests, and poll taxes, as well as physical intimidation. Over time these devices were abolished either by constitutional amendment, Acts of Congress, or Supreme Court decisions. Today women and representatives of various minority groups occupy leadership positions at every level of our nation's government.

The Fourteenth Amendment

Representative John Bingham of Ohio sat on the Joint Committee on Reconstruction, which oversaw Southern readmission into the Union; he also drafted the Fourteenth Amendment. A moderate House Republican, Bingham favored reconciliation over reprisal in dealing with the Southern states. He voted against the 1866 Civil Rights Act only because he felt Congress lacked the constitutional authority to enforce its will on the states, even for the noble cause of protecting freedmen's civil liberties. Instead, Bingham believed a constitutional amendment would be "necessary and proper" to mandate racial reform.

Bingham drafted section one of the amendment, which would grant "equal protection of the laws" to all Americans and formal citizenship to the freed slaves. He wrote this section to extend to the states the responsibility to protect those rights "chiefly defined in the first eight amendments to the Constitution of the United States."

Bingham supported the 1871 "force laws," which were enacted to protect black freedmen in the South from white terror and oppression. He believed such legislation was now constitutionally permissible under the due process clause of the Fourteenth Amendment.

Bingham remained ahead of his time in advocating the use of the Fourteenth Amendment to extend the Bill of Rights to the states. The last century of judicial interpretation has substantially realized Bingham's vision of the amendment.

JOHN BINGHAM
1815-1900

AMENDMENT XIV – SECTION 1. ALL PERSONS BORN OR NATURALIZED IN THE UNITED STATES AND SUBJECT TO THE JURISDICTION THEREOF, ARE CITIZENS OF THE UNITED STATES AND OF THE STATE WHEREIN THEY RESIDE. NO STATE SHALL MAKE OR ENFORCE ANY LAW WHICH SHALL ABRIDGE THE PRIVILEGES OR IMMUNITIES OF CITIZENS OF THE UNITED STATES; NOR SHALL ANY STATE DEPRIVE ANY PERSON OF LIFE, LIBERTY, OR PROPERTY, WITHOUT DUE PROCESS OF LAW; NOR DENY TO ANY PERSON WITHIN ITS JURISDICTION THE EQUAL PROTECTION OF THE LAW.

The Problem We All Live With
by Norman Rockwell (1964)

The Fourteenth Amendment is considered the most important change in the Constitution since the Bill of Rights because its Section 1 has been interpreted by the Supreme Court to extend to the states many of the limitations that apply to the federal government concerning individual rights. In it, for the first time, the Constitution defined national and state citizenship, to clarify that former slaves were citizens of both the United States and the states in which they lived, and to overrule the Dred Scott decision. Section 1 also prohibited states from depriving any person of life, liberty, or property "without due process of law." As interpreted, this phrase has prevented the states from interfering with many of the guarantees enumerated in the Bill of Rights.

Until the Fourteenth Amendment, the constitutional status of the Bill of Rights vis-à-vis the states had rested with the Supreme Court's decision in *Barron v. Baltimore* (1833), in which Chief Justice John Marshall had ruled that the Bill of Rights applied only to the federal government and not to the states.

Rep. John A. Bingham of Ohio, chief architect of Section 1 of the Fourteenth Amendment, said that because of the Supreme Court precedent, only a constitutional amendment could make the Bill of Rights binding on the states. Through the Fourteenth Amendment, Bingham believed that the first eight amendments, "the essential guarantees" in the Bill of Rights, would be binding on the states. He recalled James Madison's desire to include a provision prohibiting infringement by the states of certain basic rights (jury trial, freedom of religion, speech, and press).

The first legal test of the Fourteenth Amendment came in a field far removed from the purposes for which it was written. In 1869 Louisiana granted a monopoly to a slaughterhouse, effectively excluding other merchants, who sued, claiming the monopoly abridged the "privileges and immunities" guarantees of Article Four of the Constitution and the Fourteenth Amendment. In a divided opinion, the Supreme Court ruled in favor of the monopolistic practice, and in its interpretation of citizenship explained that Section 1 of the Fourteenth Amendment speaks of "privileges and immunities of citizens of the United States, and does not speak of those of citizens of the several States. . . ." Federal citizenship, according to the Court decision, involved such things as the right to vote in federal elections, the right to petition the federal government, and the right to use the navigable waters of the nation. The Court said that it was not the purpose of the Fourteenth Amendment to "transfer the security and protection of . . . civil rights . . . from the states to the Federal government." This ruling gave state governments the authority to protect many citizenship rights.

Commenting on the decision in later years, a Southern lawyer noted that the so-called *Slaughter-House Cases of 1873* ". . . marked the practical overthrow of the Congressional ideal for the Fourteenth Amendment within seven years after its victorious adop-

> *"Injustice anywhere is a threat to justice everywhere."*
> DR. MARTIN LUTHER KING, JR.

> *"[The Fourteenth Amendment] establishes equality before the law, and it gives to the humblest, the poorest, and the most despised . . . the same rights and the same protection before the law as it gives to the most powerful, the most wealthy, or the most haughty. That, sir, is republican government, as I understand it, and the only one which can claim the praise of a just government."*
> SEN. JACOB HOWARD
> (Michigan)
> May 23, 1866

tion . . . and reduced the bill of rights of Section 1 to distant potentialities."

Business corporations soon made use of the Fourteenth Amendment to claim protection against state regulations designed to control working hours and conditions. Corporations claimed a status as legal "persons" entitled to "due process" under the Fifth and Fourteenth Amendments and that attempts to regulate them abridged the "due process" clause. For more than two generations after the Civil War, such business enterprises were the only "persons" successful in claiming protection under the "due process" clause of the Fourteenth Amendment.

The "equal protection" clause of the Fourteenth Amendment suffered a grievous blow in 1896 when the Supreme Court, in *Plessy v. Ferguson,* upheld a Louisiana law requiring segregated railroad facilities. The Court said that as long as accommodations were

"Separate but Equal" 1935 (top).
Detail of the frieze of
Civil War veterans on the
Pension Building (now National Building
Museum), Washington, D.C., (bottom).

equal, blacks were not deprived of "equal protection" under the Fourteenth Amendment. The ruling established the doctrine of "separate but equal," but Justice John Harlan of Kentucky issued an eloquent dissent, arguing that "Our Constitution is color-blind, and neither knows nor tolerates classes among citizens." Blacks in many states and communities fell subject to an array of segregated institutions, including schools, hospitals, hotels, restaurants, and neighborhoods, few of them "equal."

By the late 1930s the "separate but equal" doctrine began to unravel. Missouri was ordered by the Court to admit a black student to its white law school or provide "equal" facilities. In 1950, the Court ruled that a black student in a white graduate school could not be segregated from other students. This was contrary to "equal protection of the laws," the Court said.

The "separate but equal" doctrine was dealt a death blow when the Supreme Court in 1954 ruled in *Brown v. Board of Education* that "separate but equal" segregated educational facilities were inherently "unequal." This unanimous ruling set the Court on a new course. In the years since 1954, the combination of court rulings, new federal laws, stricter enforcement of older laws, and the civil rights movement led by Dr. Martin Luther King, Jr. have substantially dismantled the walls of segregation.

The Fourteenth Amendment has now been interpreted to protect other rights against state infringement. In 1925 the Supreme Court ruled in *Gitlow v. New York* that states could not abridge First Amendment rights of free speech. The Court said, ". . . we may and do assume that freedom of speech and of the press — which are protected by the First Amendment from abridgement by Congress — are among the fundamental personal rights and liberties protected by the due process clause of the Fourteenth Amendment from impairment by the states."

The Supreme Court has made many rulings that "incorporate" First Amendment clauses into the Fourteenth Amendment. In 1961 the Court began to incorporate criminal law protections in the Fifth and Sixth Amendments into the Fourteenth Amendment, including the right to counsel and the right against self-incrimination (among them the so-called "Miranda rule" under which a suspect in custody must be read his or her rights).

These Supreme Court decisions have "nationalized" many of the provisions of the Bill of Rights. Some have been controversial because they affected deeply held opinions or reversed earlier precedents. They remind us, however, of the judiciary's primary role in applying the Constitution. "What is the service or purpose of a judiciary," John Marshall once asked, "but to execute the laws in a peaceable, orderly manner, without shedding blood, or creating a contest, or availing yourselves of force? . . . To what quarter will you look for protection from an infringement on the Constitution, if you will not give the power to the judiciary?" In the past half century the Supreme Court has led the nation toward realizing the Fourteenth Amendment's promise of equality for all Americans.

February 16, 1835   The Supreme Court rules in *Barron v. Baltimore* that the Bill of Rights is not binding on state governments.

April 14, 1873   The Supreme Court declares in the *Slaughter-House Cases* that the Fourteenth Amendment does not extend federal jurisdiction over all civil rights cases and that it was intended to protect black rights, not property rights.

March 1, 1875   Congress passes a Civil Rights Act, declaring that no U.S. citizen can be denied the use of public facilities on the basis of color. On October 15, 1883, the Supreme Court declares the Act unconstitutional.

May 10, 1886   The Supreme Court rules in *Santa Clara County v. Southern Pacific Railroad* that a corporation is a person under the Fourteenth Amendment and therefore is entitled to the same "due process" protections.

May 6, 1896   The Supreme Court declares in *Plessy v. Ferguson* that the "separate but equal" doctrine is constitutional. This decision, from which Justice John Harlan dissents, validates Jim Crow laws.

March 28, 1898   The Supreme Court rules in *United States v. Wong Kim Ark* that U.S. citizenship is without respect to race or color.

June 1, 1909   W.E.B. DuBois founds the National Association for the Advancement of Colored People.

November 25, 1915   The Ku Klux Klan is revived in Atlanta, Georgia. This organization was originally founded in 1865 in Tennessee.

June 15, 1924   The Indian Citizenship Act, granting citizenship to all Native Americans not already citizens as a result of previous legislation, is passed.

June 25, 1941   A Fair Employment Practices Committee is created by Executive Order to prevent discrimination in defense-related work.

July 26, 1948   President Truman, by Executive Order, bans segregation in U.S. Armed Forces.

May 17, 1954   The Supreme Court in *Brown v. Board of Education of Topeka* rules that "separate but equal" public schools are unconstitutional.

May 31, 1955   The Supreme Court orders desegregation of nation's schools "with all deliberate speed."

December 1, 1955   Rosa Parks is arrested for taking a seat in a "whites only" section of a Montgomery, Alabama, bus. This incident leads to Martin Luther King, Jr.'s organized boycott of Montgomery buses.

August 29, 1957   President Eisenhower signs a Civil Rights Act, establishing a Civil Rights Commission to protect voting rights.

September 4–25, 1957   President Eisenhower sends troops to Little Rock, Arkansas, to enforce court-ordered desegregation.

September 30, 1962   James Meredith is admitted to the University of Mississippi with the assistance of U.S. marshals sent by President Kennedy.

July 2, 1964
President Johnson signs a Civil Rights Act, outlawing discrimination in public accommodation, setting up the Equal Opportunity Commission, and strengthening enforcement of voting rights and integration.

May 15, 1967   In *In Re Gault,* the Supreme Court decides that a minor tried in juvenile court must be accorded most of the due process rights of an accused adult.

October 29, 1969   The Supreme Court, in *Alexander v. Holmes County Board of Education,* orders termination of all remaining segregated school systems "at once."

*"Our Constitution is color-blind, and neither knows nor tolerates classes among citizens.
In respect of civil rights, all citizens are equal before the law.
The humblest is the peer of the most powerful. The law regards man as man,
and takes no account of his surroundings or of his color
when his civil rights as guaranteed by the supreme law of the land is involved."*

JUSTICE JOHN HARLAN
dissenting opinion in *Plessy v. Ferguson*, 1896

The Nineteenth Amendment

The struggle for women's suffrage had slowed dramatically by 1916. The first generation of suffragists, women such as Elizabeth Cady Stanton, Lucretia Mott, and Susan B. Anthony, had died with their goals unachieved. At this critical juncture it was left to women like Alice Paul and Carrie Chapman Catt to rejuvenate the movement and achieve its goals.

To secure the vote throughout the nation, Catt, as president of the National American Woman Suffrage Association, proposed a "Winning Plan" — an agreement among the state leaders of the suffrage movement to bury their differences and follow Catt's directives. The two-pronged campaign concentrated on continuing agitation for suffrage in each of the states and on securing an amendment to the Constitution.

Congress passed the Nineteenth Amendment only two years after the introduction of the Winning Plan. On that occasion the entire House chamber, members and guests, broke into a spontaneous hymn of praise. Ratification by the states focused on Tennessee and a 24-year-old first-term member of the Tennessee House, Harry Burns, who kept his decision secret until the roll call. He then voted for the amendment because his mother asked him to "be a good boy and help Mrs. Catt put the 'rat' in ratification."

Looking back on the women's suffrage movement, Catt observed, "To get the word 'male' in effect out of the Constitution cost the women of this country fifty-two years of pauseless campaign."

NATIONAL PORTRAIT GALLERY

CARRIE CHAPMAN CATT
1859-1947

*T*he Nineteenth Amendment contains fewer than 50 words; yet, when it was ratified, it affected the lives of half the population of voting age and heralded victory in a struggle waged since colonial days.

The question of allowing women a voice in government was first raised in colonial Massachusetts by Anne Hutchinson, who challenged the Puritan theocracy on its position that no woman could have a vote in church affairs. Following a trial in 1637 she was banned from the Massachusetts Bay Colony.

There was a paradox in the status of colonial women. On the one hand they had fewer legal rights than men. Married women suffered "civil death," which denied them the right to own property. On the other hand, pioneer life bred a rough form of social equality between the sexes. As the American Revolution dissolved the bonds between the colonies and Britain, women like Abigail Adams began to raise the question of the woman's role in the infant republic.

During the drafting of the Declaration of Independence, Abigail Adams wrote to her husband, John Adams, advising him to "remember the ladies." The ladies were all but forgotten. Colonial voting restrictions carried over through the Declaration of Independence and the Articles of Confederation. During the framing of the Constitution, there was considerable debate over who would be eligible to vote in federal elections. Some with Gouverneur Morris wanted the vote limited to freeholders, those who owned property. Other leaders such as George Mason said that criterion would be regressive since "eight of nine states have extended the right of suffrage beyond freeholders."

In the end, the Constitution extended eligibility to vote for federal representatives to those in each state qualified to vote for members of the most numerous house of the state legislature. This left it up to the states to decide the conditions under which women could vote. For all practical purposes, however, the right to vote was limited to white males.

A turning point came with the Seneca Falls Convention of 1848, which marked the inception of the women's rights movement in the United States. The convention was the work of Elizabeth Cady Stanton and Lucretia Mott, both teachers and active abolitionists. The Convention met on July 19 and 20, 1848, and issued a Declaration of Sentiments modeled after the Declaration of Independence. It read in part "We hold these truths to be self-evident that all men and women are created equal. . . ."

By a narrow margin, the convention passed a resolution declaring "that it is the sacred duty of the women of this country to secure to themselves their sacred right to the election franchise." One signer, Charlotte Woodward, who at age 19 had been a delegate to the Seneca conference, lived to vote in the 1920 election following passage of the Nineteenth Amendment.

AMENDMENT XIX – THE RIGHT OF CITIZENS OF THE UNITED STATES TO VOTE SHALL NOT BE DENIED OR ABRIDGED BY THE UNITED STATES OR BY ANY STATE ON ACCOUNT OF SEX.

LIBRARY OF CONGRESS/IMAGEFINDERS, INC.

Suffrage parades, like this held in New York City in 1905, focused attention on the political, economic, and social inequalities women eventually overcame (above). Women today: free to choose any career (right).

© RALPH BARERRA / TEXASTOCK

"In the new code of laws which I suppose it will be necessary for you to make, I desire you would remember the ladies. . . ."

ABIGAIL ADAMS

MASSACHUSSETTS HISTORICAL SOCIETY

Following the Seneca conference, the women's rights movement worked to secure legal rights, including property rights, fair wages, and employment and educational opportunities. One of the most successful petitioners for legal rights for women was Susan B. Anthony, who became the organizational genius behind the women's rights movement. She deluged legislators with reams of petitions that got results.

As the Civil War approached, women joined anti-slavery societies and thereby learned to organize, hold public meetings, and conduct petition campaigns. The abolitionist movement gave women experience in political affairs, which they later used in pursuing their own agenda of equality.

During the Civil War, women put aside their own agenda to work for passage of the Thirteenth Amendment. Women hoped that with the emancipation of the slaves and the potential for blacks to gain the vote, their own moment also would arrive. But the Republican Party and the abolitionists had their eyes fixed solidly on Reconstruction and the freed slaves.

When women leaders learned that the provisions regarding Congressional representation in the Fourteenth Amendment used the term "male" and thereby gave the states no incentive to allow the vote for women, they were stunned. The leaders of the suffrage movement split over who would support the Fourteenth Amendment and who would oppose it. Supporters feared any modification that might endanger its passage and jeopardize the chances of blacks to gain access to political rights such as voting rights. But other suffrage leaders, like Susan B. Anthony, said they would not work to obtain the vote for blacks if women were not included and decided to pursue their own voting rights agenda.

At the same time, the women's rights movement suffered internal divisions and separated into two groups: the National Woman Suffrage Association and the American Woman Suffrage Association. They were reunited in 1890 as the National American Woman Suffrage Association. Some women's rights groups advocated getting individual state voting laws changed to include women. Others advocated an amendment to the Constitution. Their tactics also differed, ranging from demonstrations and petitions to militant picketing and hunger strikes. The strategy of gaining the vote state by state worked in the West, where women won six states. But it was not until 1913 that a state east of the Mississippi, Illinois, granted suffrage in presidential elections. New York State approved a full-suffrage amendment in 1917, bringing the number of "full suffrage" states in the Union to 11.

Following the New York victory, the stage was set to demand a constitutional amendment. By 1917 the economic and social position of women was changing rapidly, and with the advent of World War I they joined the work force in record numbers, doing work once reserved for men. Such changes made it increasingly difficult to deny women the right to vote.

The 65th Congress opened on April 1, 1917, and included the first woman to sit in the House of Representatives, Jeannette Rankin of Montana. The suffrage amendment was debated throughout the fall, and on January 9, 1918, one day before the amendment was scheduled for a vote in the House, President Woodrow Wilson removed his long-standing opposition to it. The next day the bill passed the House; 18 months later, the amendment won approval in the Senate. Despite attempts by anti-suffrage forces to defeat the measure, the amendment was ratified by the states on August 26, 1920, and 26,000,000 Americans became full-fledged citizens of the Republic.

1655 Lady Deborah Moody is permitted to vote in a Long Island, New York, town meeting, marking one of the few instances where colonial women enjoyed the franchise.

September 22, 1656 First colonial all-women jury sits in Patuxent, Maryland.

1837 Mary Lyon opens Mount Holyoke Female Seminary as first institution of higher learning for women.

February 16, 1838 Kentucky grants the right to vote in school board elections to widows who have children of school age.

July 12–19, 1848 Lucretia Mott and Elizabeth Cady Stanton organize the first women's suffrage convention at Seneca Falls, New York.

January 19, 1869 American Equal Rights Association is formed; Susan B. Anthony is elected president. On May 15, 1869, the National Woman Suffrage Association is formed with Elizabeth Cady Stanton as president.

December 10, 1869 Wyoming Territory passes the first law in the United States giving women an equal right to vote. Women, however, use the franchise for the first time on August 1, 1870 in an election in the Utah Territory.

February 18, 1890 The American and National Woman suffrage groups consolidate into the National American Woman Suffrage Association.

April 6, 1917 Jeanette Rankin (R-Montana) takes her seat as the first woman in the U.S. House of Representatives.

November 6, 1917 New York State ratifies an amendment to its constitution giving women the vote.

August 18, 1920 The Nineteenth Amendment is ratified (announced officially on August 26, 1920); the National League of Women Voters is organized that year.

Pioneers in the Women's Suffrage Movement (l to r): Elizabeth Cady Stanton (1815-1902); Susan B. Anthony (1820-1906); and Lucretia Mott (1793-1880) are featured in this statue located in the Capitol in Washington, D.C.

HARLEE LITTLE, JR.

The Twenty-Third, Twenty-Fourth and Twenty-Fifth Amendments

One of our country's greatest soldier-statesmen, President Dwight D. Eisenhower is best remembered for his leadership of the Allied Armies in World War II and for an eight-year presidency of peace and prosperity. The latter included a successful defense of the Constitution in the President's enforcement of court-ordered integration of students in Little Rock, Arkansas.

Eisenhower is less remembered for his support of the most recent amendment to the Constitution, the Twenty-sixth, giving the vote to citizens 18 years of age or older. Eisenhower's long military career and his tenure as President of Columbia University instilled in him a faith in the potential of young Americans and a desire to involve them more fully in the political process.

In his 1954 State of the Union message to Congress, President Eisenhower declared that "for years our citizens between the ages of 18 and 21 have, in time of peril, been summoned to fight for America. They should participate in the political process that produces this fateful summons."

In response to Eisenhower's message, Congress introduced a proposed amendment but it failed. In 1971, nearly two decades later, the Twenty-sixth Amendment was introduced and quickly ratified. Eisenhower did not live to see the expansion of voting rights that he helped inspire.

DWIGHT D. EISENHOWER
1890-1969

AMENDMENT XXIII – SECTION 1. THE DISTRICT CONSTITUTING THE SEAT OF GOVERNMENT OF THE UNITED STATES SHALL APPOINT IN SUCH MANNER AS THE CONGRESS MAY DIRECT:

A NUMBER OF ELECTORS OF PRESIDENT AND VICE PRESIDENT EQUAL TO THE WHOLE NUMBER OF SENATORS AND REPRESENTATIVES IN CONGRESS TO WHICH THE DISTRICT WOULD BE ENTITLED IF IT WERE A STATE, BUT IN NO EVENT MORE THAN THE LEAST POPULOUS STATE; THEY SHALL BE IN ADDITION TO THOSE APPOINTED BY THE STATES, BUT THEY SHALL BE CONSIDERED, FOR THE PURPOSES OF THE ELECTION OF PRESIDENT AND VICE PRESIDENT, TO BE ELECTORS APPOINTED BY A STATE; AND THEY SHALL MEET IN THE DISTRICT AND PERFORM SUCH DUTIES AS PROVIDED BY THE TWELFTH ARTICLE OF AMENDMENT.

AMENDMENT XXIV – SECTION 1. THE RIGHT OF CITIZENS OF THE UNITED STATES TO VOTE IN ANY PRIMARY OR OTHER ELECTION FOR PRESIDENT OR VICE PRESIDENT, FOR ELECTORS FOR PRESIDENT OR VICE PRESIDENT, OR FOR SENATOR OR REPRESENTATIVE IN CONGRESS, SHALL NOT BE DENIED OR ABRIDGED BY THE UNITED STATES OR ANY STATE BY REASON OF FAILURE TO PAY ANY POLL TAX OR OTHER TAX.

AMENDMENT XXVI – SECTION 1. THE RIGHT OF CITIZENS OF THE UNITED STATES, WHO ARE EIGHTEEN YEARS OF AGE OR OLDER, TO VOTE SHALL NOT BE DENIED OR ABRIDGED BY THE UNITED STATES OR BY ANY STATE ON ACCOUNT OF AGE.

D.C. PUBLIC LIBRARY, WASHINGTONIANA DIVISION

The view of the Capitol and Pennsylvania Avenue, seen from the roof of the White House, is recorded in an 1839 handtinted engraving (above). Voter registration drive on campus (right).

*W*ith the extension of voting rights to residents of the District of Columbia and to 18-year-olds and with the elimination of the poll tax, suffrage in America became nearly universal, and the country took a major step toward fully realizing the ideal of equality for all its citizens.

Of these three final amendments in the voting rights saga, the Twenty-sixth Amendment granting suffrage to 18-year-olds won the quickest acceptance. The fact that the Vietnam War and the draft were at their height perhaps served to accelerate the process.

For years many political leaders, including President Dwight D. Eisenhower and Senator Jennings Randolph of West Virginia, had called for the measure. Congress wanted to allow these young people a voice in government and believed the way to do it was through an amendment to the Voting Rights Act of 1965, which would have expired in 1970. The act suspended literacy, educational, and character tests of voter qualifications. The issue did not have to do with the extension itself or with granting the vote to younger Americans. Rather, it centered on the power of Congress to change state-established age qualifications for voting. Article I, Section 2 of the Constitution states that the electors in each state for House of Representatives "shall have the same qualifications requisite for electors of the most numerous branch of the state legislature. . . ." Many in and out of government believed that this clause delegated to the states the right to determine voting age qualifications.

In the opinion of the Department of Justice, Congressional power in the area was "uncertain and dubious." Although President Richard M. Nixon favored extending both the vote to 18-year-olds and the Voting Rights Act, he believed an amendment to the Constitution was necessary to achieve the vote for 18-year-olds.

In the end, both Houses of Congress accepted a lower voting age in the Voting Rights Act with the understanding that its constitutionality would be judged by the Supreme Court. The act was immediately challenged, and the Court ruled in 1970 that although Congress had the power to lower the voting age in federal elections, this power did not extend to state and local elections.

The Court's decision threatened to throw the 1972 national and state elections into chaos, because in most states the voting age for choosing federal officials would have been different from the voting age for state races.

Congress reacted quickly with the Twenty-sixth Amendment. Beyond the legal urgencies created by the Court's decision, many had come to believe that if 18-year-olds were considered adults under certain laws and were mature enough to fight and to sacrifice their lives for their country, they should be given the opportunity to express their views through the ballot box. The Twenty-sixth Amendment sailed through Congress and was ratified by the states

in just 107 days, the shortest time ever required to complete the amending process. As a result, 11,000,000 Americans between the ages of 18 and 21 were enfranchised.

Granting the vote to residents of the District of Columbia had proved not as easy. Agitation for such a measure dated to 1801, just 11 years after the District was created, and some form of Congressional action had been requested every year since then. District residents wanted representation in the Congress and the vote to make this possible. Opponents of suffrage for the District feared that voting rights would lead to agitation for statehood, diminishing the power of the Congress over the "federal city."

From the beginning, the District and its residents had been a national and constitutional anomaly. The District was designated by the Residence Act of 1790, which made it the nation's capital. In its early years, the District was administered by a mayor appointed by the President. An 1820 law provided for the direct election of the mayor. In 1871 Congress established a municipal government for the District with a governor and council appointed by the President. As the District assumed more control over its affairs, its residents became insistent on the right to vote and to be represented in the national government.

Finally, in 1960 Congress proposed the Twenty-third Amendment, which was ratified in less than a year. The amendment was a compromise. While it permitted District citizens to choose presidential electors who would participate in electing the President and Vice President, it did not give the District delegates in Congress. Later, Congress authorized the District a nonvoting representative in Congress.

The amendment did not give the District any other attributes of a state or change the constitutional powers of the Congress to legislate with respect to the District and to prescribe its form of government. The amendment allowed the District no more electoral votes than the least populous state, thus for practical purposes fixing the District's electoral votes at three.

The third of these constitutional extensions of the franchise came about with the passage of the Twenty-fourth Amendment, a result of the civil rights struggles of the 1960s. The amendment abolished the poll tax as a qualification for voting in national elections, ending one of the last legal barriers to the polling place and making a reality of the Fifteenth Amendment.

The poll tax had been used primarily in southern states as a qualification for voting. The tax was generally $2, and some counties added another $1 to vote in local elections. This was the equivalent of a day's pay. Sometimes politicians paid the tax for whites, but even those blacks who could afford the tax were often coerced into not paying it.

In 1962 Congressional testimony, a black southern minister said that the black population in his county was 7,643, yet not one of these citizens was registered to vote. The minister explained that the poll tax had to be paid at the sheriff's office by January before

Washington, D.C. residents in line to become among the first to register to vote.

citizens could vote in upcoming elections. He said that the sheriff told blacks, "don't come to the court house and try to pay taxes before the first day of February."

Along with poll taxes, the Twenty-fourth Amendment prohibited other taxes, because witnesses said that if the poll tax alone were mentioned in the amendment, "such devices as a personal property tax on automobiles might be imposed to take its place."

In 1964, when the Twenty-fourth Amendment was ratified, only five states retained payment of the poll tax as a voting qualification. Even after its passage, four states, distinguishing national from local elections, continued to levy a poll tax for voting in state elections. Two years after the amendment, the Supreme Court ruled in *Harper v. Virginia Board of Elections* that conditioning the right to vote on payment of a tax violated the equal protection clause of the Fourteenth Amendment. This ruling effectively abolished the poll tax in both national and state elections.

These extensions of the "power of the ballot box" by the Constitution have worked to transform the nation's life — changing old political alignments, transforming many state and local governments, and striking down remaining barriers of injustice. As Senator Everett Dirksen of Illinois said of the 1964 Civil Rights Bill, passed in the same year as the Twenty-fourth Amendment, "Every denial of freedom, every denial of equal opportunity for a livelihood, for an education, for the right to participate in representative government diminishes me. There is the moral basis for our cause."

The editors wish to acknowledge their indebtedness, in preparing the list of historical dates in this book, to Arthur M. Schlesinger, Jr., ed. *The Almanac of American History* (New York, 1983), Calvin D. Linton, ed. *The Bicentennial Almanac: 200 Years of America* (Nashville, New York, 1975), and other sources included in the bibliography.

July 16, 1790 President Washington signs legislation establishing the District of Columbia as the national capital, beginning in 1800. Philadelphia is chosen as the interim seat of government.

July 16, 1791 Black mathematician and scientist Benjamin Banneker submits his plans for the nation's new capital in Washington, D.C.

June 1800 The federal capital moves from Philadelphia to Washington, D.C.

June 20, 1818 Connecticut becomes the first eastern state to remove property qualifications for voting.

October 1841 The "Dorr Rebellion" in Rhode Island begins, demanding a more liberal franchise; a new state constitution is adopted in April 1843.

January 31, 1867 Congress grants suffrage to all males 21 years of age or older in all U.S. territories.

June 11, 1878 The District of Columbia receives a permanent constitution from Congress.

April 3, 1944 The Supreme Court rules in *Smith v. Allwright* that a person cannot be denied the right to vote in a party primary on the grounds of race.

March 29, 1961 The Twenty-third Amendment, granting the vote in presidential elections to the District of Columbia, is ratified.

January 23, 1964 The Twenty-fourth Amendment, removing economic restrictions on voting, is ratified.

August 6, 1965 The Voting Rights Act of 1965, abolishing literacy requirements and extending to Native Americans all protections granted non-native English-speaking citizens, is passed.

March 24, 1966 The Supreme Court rules in *Harper v. Virginia Board of Elections* that poll tax requirements in state elections violate the equal protection clause of the Fourteenth Amendment.

July 1, 1971 The Twenty-sixth Amendment, granting the franchise to all citizens 18 years or older, is ratified.

May 7, 1974 By referendum, citizens of the District of Columbia accept the home rule charter passed by Congress on December 24, 1973.

1987-1991

THE BICENTENNIAL OF OUR CONSTITUTION AND BILL OF RIGHTS OCCURS IN MOMENTOUS TIMES,

with the human urge for freedom breaking out all over the world. One after another, repressive governments have toppled as their people reached for those basic rights we in this country have enjoyed for more than 200 years. Historians may someday refer to these times as the "Epoch of Human Rights." Human energy and ideas may be surpressed and contained by brute force but like a volcano they will ultimately erupt. Ever since people left their crude dwellings in caves and trees and began living in tribes and villages, they have had to reconcile liberty with order. They swiftly learned that individual freedom had to be balanced with the common need for security.

HARLEE LITTLE, JR.

Man Controlling Trade, *a metaphor for man controlling governmental power, sculpted by Michael Lantz, stands outside the Federal Trade Commission in Washington, D.C.*

Those who wrote our Constitution in 1787 and the Bill of Rights which followed did not invent all the great ideas and values those documents embraced. They drew upon the wisdom of the ages to combine the best ideals of the past in a concept of government of "We the People," with the Bill of Rights added to provide defined limits on that government to make sure to protect individual rights.

This Constitution was not perfect in 1787; it is not perfect today even with its amendments, but it has continued to provide ordered liberty longer than any other written document of government in all history. It sought to fulfill the promises of the Declaration of Independence of 1776 that so eloquently expressed peoples' yearning to be free to develop their God-given talents. Three separate, independent branches of our government were devised to provide for checks and balances to keep powers of government within the boundaries set by the fundamental law. The average American of that day could grasp the meaning of the first ten amendments better than the nuances of separation of powers. Taken as a whole, the Constitution provided the powers needed to govern, while the Bill of Rights gave assurance that those protections of individual freedom would serve as a harness on that governmental power. It gave comfort to the people who remembered how the monarchical powers of national governments had suppressed individual freedoms in Europe. Dependent as they were, literally, on "horse power," they knew that the value of a horse lay in having it in harness.

For 200 years this system of government has unleashed the energies and talents of a whole people to create a good life for most. Except as to fundamental values, it provides no rigid blueprint that fits all people in all lands; each must discover its own course. But the American experience offers an inspiring example of ageless ideals realized and made to work, and a reminder that men and women everywhere were intended by their Creator to be free to carve out their own destinies. Henry Steele Commager said well, "Nothing in all history ever succeeded like America." Our duty is to make sure to pass on this achievement to succeeding generations.

Warren E. Burger

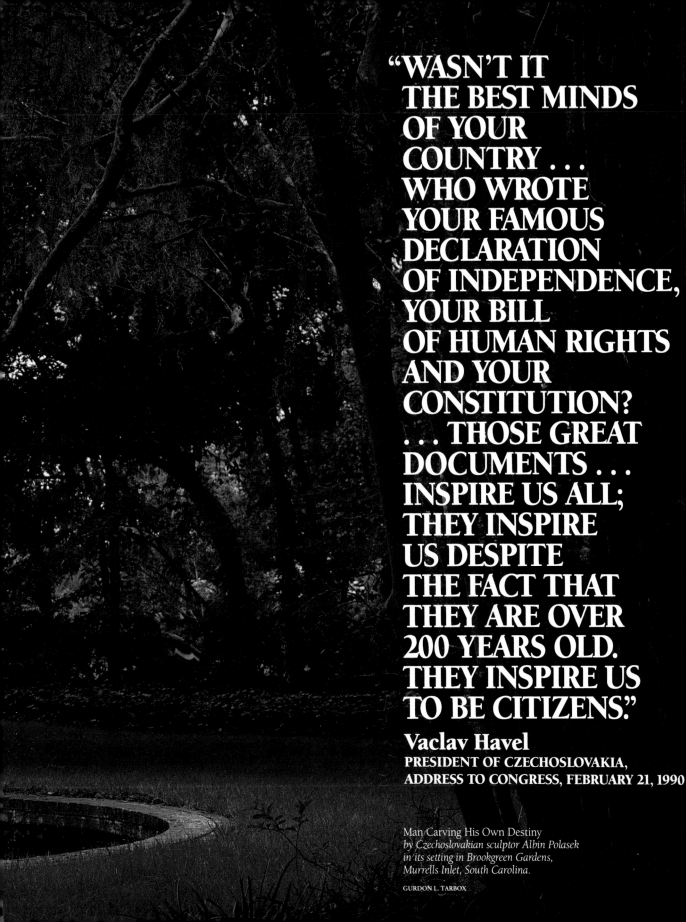

"WASN'T IT THE BEST MINDS OF YOUR COUNTRY ... WHO WROTE YOUR FAMOUS DECLARATION OF INDEPENDENCE, YOUR BILL OF HUMAN RIGHTS AND YOUR CONSTITUTION? ... THOSE GREAT DOCUMENTS ... INSPIRE US ALL; THEY INSPIRE US DESPITE THE FACT THAT THEY ARE OVER 200 YEARS OLD. THEY INSPIRE US TO BE CITIZENS."

Vaclav Havel
**PRESIDENT OF CZECHOSLOVAKIA,
ADDRESS TO CONGRESS, FEBRUARY 21, 1990**

Man Carving His Own Destiny
*by Czechoslovakian sculptor Albin Polasek
in its setting in Brookgreen Gardens,
Murrells Inlet, South Carolina.*

GURDON L. TARBOX

Note to Teachers and Librarians

This book has been produced by the Commission on the Bicentennial of the United States Constitution as an educational resource to help you convey to students a history and civics lesson about our nation's constitutional heritage and its significance in our daily lives. The following suggestions may assist you in planning classroom activities, special school exhibits or events, and other educational experiences.

WEST PARK, DELAWARE

Discuss the term **Bill of Rights.** Begin by having students consider the meaning of the words "bill" and "rights." Ask students to identify different kinds of rights, such as natural, civil, political, economic, etc. Have students research the common understanding of the term "rights" today as compared with those in earlier eras and centuries, e.g., the Magna Carta.

The list of **historical dates** included in the discussion of each right provides material for the start of a historical timeline. Students could also be encouraged to consider the connection between the dates and the rights in question. For example, what has John Brown's raid on Harper's Ferry to do with the Thirteenth-Fifteenth Amendments?

Historical illustrations offer an excellent opportunity for younger students to examine the visual differences in American society from the past to the present. This book includes a number of illustrations showing the origins and current applications of particular rights. Students could be encouraged to study, analyze, and explain the meaning of this graphic material in terms of its literal and symbolic meanings.

Encourage students to read **biographies** of men or women well known as leaders in the struggle for American rights, some of whom are featured in this book. Have students select a person associated with a claim of rights and encourage them to investigate the factors in that person's life that explain how that person developed a commitment to the right in question and was prepared to act on that commitment. As a class assignment, ask students to prepare a "Hall of Fame" for Americans and for men and women of other nations who contributed to human rights; ask students to prepare a "citation" honoring each individual selected.

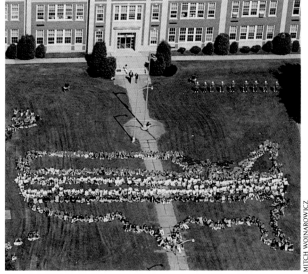

MITCH WOJNAROWICZ

Have students read the **quotations** on rights selected for this book. Consider the meaning in terms of who said them and why. Note the historical context of a quotation. What conclusions can be drawn from this? Are there other quotations on rights that either you or the student can think of?

Use **choral reading** to introduce a class to the various amendments in the Bill of Rights (hearing the amendment, as well as seeing it, makes a deeper impression and may lead to a deeper involvement in searching for its meaning). This may be done as a general classroom activity with specific students then assigned the task of researching and discussing a particular right or amendment.

Have students **research their local history** for examples of rights that have had a direct impact on their community. Have them look at famous cases that began in their state or locality. Where appropriate, ask them to focus on their own state's role in adopting the Bill of Rights. A study of the immediate precedents of our national Bill of Rights would lead students to consider the relationship between their state's bill of rights and the national Bill of Rights.

Have students **take a particular right and follow its historical roots** as far back as possible. For example, historically, the right to be spared excessive bail is one of the basic legal protections drawn upon by anyone who stands charged with a crime and who faces imprisonment unless bail is paid. Ask students to determine why a particular right was considered important enough to be included in the Bill of Rights.

Ask students to arrange the Bill of Rights in order of what they consider to be the **priority of importance of its various rights in today's world.** Ask them to justify their evaluations.

Rights represent different ideals or principles. For instance, the rights in our Constitution can be interpreted as representing the ideals of liberty, justice, and equality. Ask students to study the various provisions in the Bill of Rights and subsequent amendments and categorize them according to these **primary ideals.**

Encourage students to **read and interpret important historical documents** — e.g., the Mayflower Compact — to determine what they meant in their time and what they tell us by way of implication about the age that produced them. Ask students to rewrite these documents in their own words.

Study with students the **effectiveness of claims of rights.** The following are some questions and statements that could be considered: How can a society assure the implementation of a claim of rights once it is entered or agreed to? What enabling mechanism is needed? What happens when it is absent? James Madison called

Annual Constitution Day Parade, Nevada City, California (next page).

JOHN R. HART, "THE UNION"

WASHINGTON, D.C.

constitutional guarantees without such mechanisms mere "parchment barriers." What sorts of practical guarantees are needed to make such a document effective? What institutions in our government have become the guardians of our rights?

Ask students to examine the **relationship between rights and responsibilities.** In what ways does our enjoyment of rights depend on our assuming certain responsibilities as citizens?

The political process of drafting the American Bill of Rights and similar documents has interested many scholars. Students can research materials to find out who favored and who opposed the particular claim of rights, and what were the pro and con arguments. Arrange for a debate in class between the **Federalist and Anti-Federalist positions** on the desirability of incorporating a bill of rights in the Constitution.

Assign to students a **comparison of the U.S. Bill of Rights with rights guarantees in other countries** (e.g., England, USSR, or Canada). Ask them to identify the major similarities and differences and to determine the influence one document may have had on another. Students can also be given the opportunity to compare the rights in our Bill of Rights with the U.N. Universal Declaration of Human Rights.

Have students **investigate the causes of racial and sex discrimination.** For example, ask them to discuss the status of women in this country and in many other parts of the world. Reading current newspapers, students can find stories related to minority rights that might have been unheard of two hundred years ago.

Ask students to consider **minority vs. majority rights** as they are known today and have been realized in the past. What is meant by the "tyranny of the majority" as that relates to the application of the Bill of Rights? Ask students to consider how our commitment to democracy might conflict with our commitment to the rights of the individual.

Build and bury a **time capsule** containing 1991 Bicentennial memorabilia to be unearthed in fifty or one hundred years.

Hold a **film festival** on Bill of Rights themes. Films such as *Twelve Angry Men, To Kill a Mockingbird, Mississippi Burning, The Ox-Bow Incident,* and *The Crucible* could be included.

KEN WOODLEY

Assign students to write reports on topics related to the Bill of Rights that are of historical, current, or personal interest. Conduct a **school essay contest** on a Bill of Rights theme, e.g., what if the Bill of Rights and its subsequent amendments had not become a part of our Constitution? Ask students to write a paper on what effect the lack of a Bill of Rights would have on American citizens today, or investigate issues concerning the right to privacy, freedom of speech, rights of the accused, and the

right to bear arms. Throughout the school and community, sponsor **art, essay, photography, and historical/pictorial map contests** with a Bill of Rights theme.

Encourage students to **design trivia questions, quizzes, and crossword puzzles** on the Bill of Rights.

Have students dramatize, through the use of **plays and dramatic readings,** the meaning of the *Bill of Rights and Beyond.* Assist students in writing original scripts of their own on the Bill of Rights.

Have students select a novel or non-fiction book concerning rights and prepare a **book review and/or oral report** to the class.

Plan a Bicentennial **Bill of Rights bookshelf display;** encourage students to refer to the many books available on the Bill of Rights. Arrange a media center display on the Bill of Rights, including movies, filmstrips, videos, records, etc.

Design **field trips,** with a Bill of Rights focus, to a court house, police station, or historical site.

Invite speakers to address the classroom or an assembly, presenting information on the Bill of Rights and subsequent amendments such as the Civil War amendments (13, 14, 15) or the suffrage amendments (19, 24, 26). Invite recently naturalized citizens to school to speak on the differences between rights enjoyed in the United States and those in their native country.

Take advantage of assembly programs and **special days or months in the school calendar** to stage special events and learning activities on the Bill of Rights (e.g., Law Day, Women's History Month, Black History Month).

Have students participate in **mock trial** presentations of landmark Supreme Court cases specifically concerned with Bill of Rights issues.

Assign students to design **eye-catching ads** on the Bill of Rights with the purpose of encouraging public interest and understanding of the *Bill of Rights and Beyond.* Conduct a **school poster contest** on a Bill of Rights theme. Encourage local stores to display the winning posters. Ask students to design a **cartoon,** a **stamp,** or an appropriate **symbol or logo** on a Bill of Rights topic.

Work with students to create a **scrapbook** of current newspaper and magazine articles and their photographs dealing with Bill of Rights issues.

Design a **"town/gown" forum** on the Bill of Rights and related topics.

Arrange for students to **attend a meeting of the city council, school board, or other government bodies.** Discuss the content and procedures of the meeting.

Have students prepare a **bulletin board** on the amendments that deal with specific topics of interest, such as black issues, women, and suffrage.

Assign students to **write a poem or compose a song** expressing their feelings about the rights guaranteed American citizens under the Constitution.

Assign students to **draft a press release** about the celebration of the Bill of Rights in their school.

Passing a Legacy by Louis Glanzman (next page).
COURTESY OF LIBERTY BELL FOUNDATION HEADQUARTERS, FORT WASHINGTON, PENNSYLVANIA

Selected Bibliography*

HARLEE LITTLE, JR

The U. S. Constitution

Adams, Willi P. *The First American Constitutions: Republican Ideology and the Making of State Constitutions in the Revolutionary Era.* (Chapel Hill, North Carolina, 1980).

Adler, Mortimer. *We Hold These Truths.* (New York, 1987).

Allen, W. B. and Gordon Lloyd, eds. *The Essential Anti-Federalist.* (Lanham, Maryland, 1985).

Bailyn, Bernard. *The Ideological Origins of the American Revolution.* (Cambridge, Massachusetts, 1972).

Barbash, Fred. *The Founding: A Dramatic Account of the Writing of the Constitution.* (New York, 1987).

Berns, Walter. *Taking the Constitution Seriously.* (New York, 1987).

Bickel, Alexander M. *The Least Dangerous Branch: The Supreme Court at the Bar of Politics.* (New Haven, Connecticut, 1986).

Bickford, Charlene Bangs and Kenneth R. Bowling. *Birth of a Nation: The Federal Congress, 1789-1791.* (Madison, Wisconsin, 1989).

Bloom, Allan, ed. *Confronting the Constitution.* (Washington, D.C., 1990).

Bowen, Catherine Drinker. *Miracle at Philadelphia.* (Boston, 1966).

Burger, Warren E. *The Constitution: Foundation of Our Freedom.* (Orlando, Florida, 1990).

Carr, William G. *The Oldest Delegate.* (Newark, Delaware, 1990).

Collier, Christopher and James Lincoln Collier. *Decision at Philadelphia: The Constitutional Convention of 1787.* (New York, 1986).

Conley, Patrick T. and John P. Kaminski, eds. *The Constitution and the States: The Role of the Original Thirteen in the Framing and Adoption of the Federal Constitution.* (Madison, Wisconsin, 1988).

Conley, Patrick T. and Albert T. Klyberg. *Rhode Island's Road to Liberty.* (Providence, 1987).

Cooke, Jacob E. *Alexander Hamilton: A Biography.* (New York, 1982).

Corwin, Edward S. *The Constitution and What It Means Today.* (Princeton, New Jersey, 1978).

Crosskey, William Winslow. *Politics and the Constitution.* (Chicago, 1980).

Currie, David P. *The Constitution in the Supreme Court: The First One Hundred Years.* (Chicago, 1985).

Diamond, Martin. *The Founding of the Democratic Republic.* (Itasca, Illinois, 1981).

Farrand, Max, ed. *The Records of the Federal Convention of 1787.* (New Haven, 1987).

Feinberg, Barbara Silberdick. *The Constitution: Yesterday, Today, and Tomorrow.* (New York, 1987).

Ferris, Robert G. and James H. Charleton. *The Signers of the Constitution.* (Arlington, Virginia, 1986).

Friendly, Fred W. and Martha J.H. Elliot. *The Constitution: That Delicate Balance.* (New York, 1984).

Garraty, John A., ed. *Quarrels That Have Shaped the Constitution.* (New York, 1975).

Goldman, Sheldon. *Constitutional Law: Cases and Essays.* (New York, 1987).

Goldwin, Robert A. and William Schambra, eds. *How Does the Constitution Secure Rights?* (Washington, D.C., 1985).

Graham, Fred P. *The Due Process Revolution: The Warren Court's Impact on Criminal Law.* (Rochelle Park, New Jersey, 1970).

Hall, Kermit. *A Comprehensive Bibliography of American Constitutional and Legal History.* 5 vols. (Millwood, New York, 1984).

Hamilton, Alexander, James Madison and John Jay. *The Federalist Papers.* (New York, 1788).

Hyman, Harold and William M. Wiecek. *Equal Justice Under Law: Constitutional Development, 1835-1875.* (New York, 1982).

Jensen, Merrill et al., eds. *The Documentary History of the Ratification of the Constitution.* (Madison, Wisconsin, 1976-1984).

Josephy, Alvin M., Jr. *History of the Congress of the United States.* (New York, 1975).

*This list is illustrative of educational resources on the constitutional period, the Bill of Rights, and rights in general and does not carry with it any endorsement by the Commission of any specific titles or their points of view.

Kammen, Michael. *A Machine That Would Go of Itself: The Constitution in American Culture.* (New York, 1986).

Kammen, Michael. *The Origins of the American Constitution: A Documentary History.* (New York, 1986).

Kelly, Alfred, Winfred Harbison, and Herman Belz. *The American Constitution: Its Origins and Development.* (New York, 1983).

Ketcham, Ralph L. *James Madison: A Biography.* (New York, 1971).

Ketcham, Ralph L., ed. *The Anti-Federalist Papers and the Constitutional Convention Debates.* (New York, 1987).

Kurland, Phillip B. and Ralph Lerner, eds. *The Founders' Constitution.* (Chicago, 1987).

Levy, Leonard W., Kenneth L. Karst, and Dennis J. Mahoney, eds. *The Encyclopedia of the American Constitution.* (New York, 1986).

Madison, James, ed. Adrienne Koch. *Notes of Debates in the Federal Convention of 1787.* (Athens, Ohio, 1985).

McCarrick, Earlean M., ed. *U.S. Constitution: A Guide to Information Sources.* (Detroit, 1980).

McDonald, Forrest. *Novus Ordo Seclorum: The Intellectual Origins of the Constitution.* (Lawrence, Kansas, 1985).

McGee, Dorothy Horton. *Framers of the Constitution.* (New York, 1987).

Mee, Charles L. Jr. *The Genius of the People.* (New York, 1987).

Morgan, Edmund S. *Inventing the People: The Rise of Popular Sovereignty in England and America.* (New York, 1988).

Morris, Richard B. *The Framing of the Federal Constitution.* (Washington, D.C., 1986).

Morris, Richard B. *Witnesses at the Creation: Hamilton, Madison, Jay and the Constitution.* (New York, 1985).

O'Connor, Thomas and Alan Rogers. *This Momentous Affair: Massachusetts and the Ratification of the U.S. Constitution.* (Boston, 1987).

Onuf, Peter S. *Statehood and Union: A History of the Northwest Ordinance.* (Bloomington, Indiana, 1987).

Padover, Saul K., revised by Jacob W. Landynski. *The Living U.S. Constitution.* (New York, 1982).

Peck, Robert S. *We The People: The Constitution in American Life.* (New York, 1987).

Peltason, J. W. *Understanding the Constitution.* (New York, 1985).

Peters, William. *A More Perfect Union: The Men and Events That Made the Constitution.* (New York, 1987).

Preiss, Byron and David Osterlund, eds. *The Constitution of the United States of America.* (New York, 1987).

Read, Conyers, ed. *The Constitution Reconsidered.* (New York, 1968).

Redenius, Charles. *The American Ideal of Equality: From Jefferson's Declaration to the Burger Court.* (New York, 1981).

Reid, John Phillip. *In Defiance of the Law: The Standing-Army Controversy, the Two Constitutions, and the Coming of the American Revolution.* (Chapel Hill, 1981).

Rehnquist, William H. *The Supreme Court: How It Was, How It Is.* (New York, 1987).

Richards, David A.J. *Toleration and the Constitution.* (New York, 1986).

Rodell, Fred. *55 Men: The Story of the Constitution.* (Harrisburg, 1986).

Rossiter, Clinton. *1787: The Grand Convention.* (New York, 1966).

Rutland, Robert. *The Ordeal of the Constitution: The Anti-Federalists and the Ratification Struggle of 1787-88.* (Boston, 1983).

Schechter, Stephen L. and Richard B. Bernstein, eds. *Well Begun: Chronicles of the Early National Period.* (Albany, 1989).

St. John, Jeffrey. *Constitutional Journal: A Correspondent's Report from the Convention of 1787.* (Ottawa, Illinois, 1987).

St. John, Jeffrey. *A Child of Fortune: A Correspondent's Report on the Ratification of the U.S. Constitution & the Battle for a Bill of Rights.* (Ottawa, Illinois, 1990).

Storing, Herbert J., ed. *The Complete Anti-Federalist: Writings by the Opponents of the Constitution.* (Chicago, 1985).

Urofsky, Melvin I. *A March of Liberty: A Constitutional History of the United States.* (New York, 1988).

Van Doren, Carl. *The Great Rehearsal.* (Westport, Connecticut, 1982).

Vetterli, Richard and Gary Bryner. *In Search of the Republic: Public Virtue and the Roots of American Government.* (Totowa, New Jersey, 1987).

Wheeler, Everett Pepperell. *Daniel Webster, The Expounder of the Constitution.* (Littleton, Colorado, 1986).

Detail of the pediment of the National Archives building (top left).

Wood, Gordon S. *The Creation of the American Republic, 1776-1787.* (New York, 1972).

Wright, Edmond. *Franklin of Philadelphia.* (Cambridge, Massachusetts, 1986).

The U.S. Bill of Rights and Subsequent Amendments

Abraham, Henry J. *Freedom and the Court: Civil Rights and Liberties in the United States.* (New York, 1988).

Adams, Arlin M. *A Nation Dedicated to Religious Liberty: The Constitutional Heritage of the Religion Clauses.* (Philadelphia, 1990).

Alderman, Ellen and Caroline Kennedy. *In Our Defense: The Bill of Rights in Action.* (New York, 1991).

Alley, Robert S., ed. *James Madison on Religious Liberty.* (New York, 1985).

Baer, Judith A. *Equality Under the Constitution: Reclaiming the Fourteenth Amendment.* (New York, 1983).

Baker, Leonard. *John Marshall: A Life in Law.* (Norwalk, Connecticut, 1990).

Barlow, J. Jackson, Dennis J. Mahoney, and John G. West, eds. *The New Federalist Papers.* (Lanham, Maryland, 1988).

Belz, Herman. *Emancipation and Equal Rights: Politics and Constitutionalism in the Civil War Era.* (New York, 1978).

Berns, Walter. *The First Amendment and the Future of American Democracy.* (Chicago, 1985).

The Bill of Rights. Washington, D.C.: National Archives & Records Administration, 1986.

Bollinger, Lee C. *Images of a Free Press.* (Chicago, 1991).

Bowling, Kenneth R. "'A Tub to the Whale': The Founding Fathers and the Adoption of the Federal Bill of Rights," *Journal of the Early Republic.* (New York, 1988).

Brant, Irving. *The Bill of Rights: Its Origin and Meaning.* (Indianapolis, 1965).

Burger, Warren E. "The Bill of Rights: What It Means To Us," *Parade Magazine.* (New York, 1991).

Canavan, Francis. *Freedom of Expression: Purpose As Limit.* (Durham, North Carolina, 1984).

Carter, T. Barton, Mark A. Franklin, and Jay B. Wright. *The First Amendment and the Fourth Estate; The Law of Mass Media.* (Westbury, New York, 1988).

Chafee, Zechariah, Jr. *Free Speech in the United States.* (New York, 1961).

Cortner, Richard C. *The Supreme Court and the Second Bill of Rights: The Fourteenth Amendment and the Nationalization of Civil Liberties.* (Madison, Wisconsin, 1981).

Curry, Thomas J. *The First Freedoms: Church and State in America to the Passage of the First Amendment.* (New York, 1986).

Dorsey, Gray L. *American Freedom: A Bicentennial Essay on the Bill of Rights.* (New York, 1987).

Emerson, Thomas I. *The System of Freedom of Expression.* (New York, 1970).

Haiman, Franklyn S., ed. *To Protect These Rights.* (Skokie, Illinois, 1976).

Haiman, Franklyn S. *Speech and Law in a Free Society.* (Chicago, 1981).

Hand, Learned. *The Bill of Rights.* (Cambridge, Massachusetts, 1962).

Henkin, Louis. *The Age of Rights.* (New York, 1990).

The History of the Bill of Rights. (Englewood Cliffs, New Jersey, 1991).

Hutson, James H. "The Birth of the Bill of Rights: The State of Current Scholarship," *Prologue: Quarterly of the National Archives.* (Washington, D.C., 1988).

James, Joseph B. *The Ratification of the Fourteenth Amendment.* (Macon, Georgia, 1984).

Ketcham, Ralph L. "The Dilemma of Bills of Rights in Democratic Government," in *The Legacy of George Mason.* (Fairfax, Virginia, 1983).

Kluger, Richard. *Simple Justice: The History of Brown v. Board of Education and Black America's Struggle for Equality.* (New York, 1975).

Korvitz, Milton R. *Bill of Rights Reader: Leading Constitutional Cases.* (Ithaca, New York, 1973).

Levy, Leonard W. *Emergence of a Free Press.* (New York, 1985).

Levy, Leonard W. *The Establishment Clause: Religion and the First Amendment.* (New York, 1986).

Levy, Leonard W. *Origins of the 5th Amendment: The Right Against Self-Incrimination.* (New York, 1968).

Lieberman, Jethro K. *The Enduring Constitution: An Exploration of the First 200 Years.* (New York, 1987).

McCloskey, Herbert and Alida Brill. *Dimensions of Tolerance: What Americans Believe about Civil Liberties.* (New York, 1983).

McNeil, Genna Rae. *Groundwork: Charles Hamilton Houston and the Struggle for Civil Rights.* (Philadelphia, 1983).

Neely, Mark E., Jr. *The Fate of Liberty: Abraham Lincoln and Civil Liberties.* (New York, 1990).

Peck, Robert S. *The Bill of Rights and the Politics of Interpretation.* (St. Paul, 1991).

Peck, Robert S., ed. *Speaking and Writing Truth: Community Forums on the First Amendment.* (Chicago, 1985).

Peterson, Merrill D. *Thomas Jefferson and the New Nation: A Biography.* (New York, 1970).

Rutland, Robert Allen. *The Birth of the Bill of Rights, 1776-1791.* (Boston, 1983).

Sandoz, Ellis. *Conceived in Liberty: American Individual Rights Today.* (North Scituate, Massachusetts, 1978).

Schechter, Stephen L. and Richard B. Bernstein, eds. *Contexts of the Bill of Rights.* (Albany, 1990).

Schwartz, Bernard. *The Bill of Rights: A Documentary History.* (New York, 1971).

Schwartz, Bernard. *The Great Rights of Mankind: A History of the American Bill of Rights.* (New York, 1977).

Starr, Isidore. *The Idea of Liberty: First Amendment Freedoms.* (St. Paul, 1978).

Starr, Isidore. *Justice: Due Process of Law.* (St. Paul, 1981).

Tedford, Thomas L. *Freedom of Speech in the United States.* (Carbondale, Illinois, 1985).

Other Works

Anthony, Katherine Susan. *Susan B. Anthony: Her Personal History and Era.* (New York, 1954).

Arbetman, Lee and Richard Roe. *Great Trials in American History, Civil War to the Present.* (Minneapolis, 1985).

Armstrong, Virginia, ed. *I Have Spoken: American History Through the Voices of the Indians.* (Chicago, 1971).

Aymar, Brandt and Edward Sagarin. *Laws and Trials That Created History.* (New York, 1974).

Bailyn, Bernard. *Faces of Revolution: Personalities and Themes in the Struggle for American Independence.* (New York, 1990).

Barry, Kathleen. *Susan B. Anthony, A Biography.* (New York, 1988).

Bennett, Lerone, Jr. *Before the Mayflower: A History of Black America.* (New York, 1984).

Berkhofer, Robert F. Jr. *The White Man's Indian: Images of the American Indian from Columbus to the Present.* (New York, 1978).

Branson, Margaret S. and Judith Torney-Purta, eds. *International Human Rights, Society and the Schools.* Bulletin 68. (Washington, D.C., 1982).

Brown, Dee Alexander. *Bury My Heart at Wounded Knee: An Indian History of the American West.* (New York, 1970).

Brown, Richard D. *Massachusetts, A Bicentennial History.* (New York, 1978).

Brownlie, Ian, ed. *Basic Documents on Human Rights.* (Oxford, 1971).

Buergenthal, Thomas and Judith V. Torney. *International Human Rights and International Education.* (Washington, D.C., 1976).

Chrimes, S. B. *English Constitutional History.* (Oxford, 1953).

Claude, Richard P., ed. *Comparative Human Rights.* (Baltimore and London, 1976).

Conta, Marcia Maher. *Women for Human Rights.* (Milwaukee, 1979).

DePauw, Linda Grant. *Founding Mothers: Women of America in the Revolutionary Era.* (Boston, 1975).

Douglas, William O. *An Almanac of Liberty.* (New York, 1954).

Douglass, Frederick. *Narrative of the Life of Frederick Douglass.* (New York, 1968).

Douglass, Frederick. *Thoughts for All Time.* (Washington, D.C., 1984).

DuBois, Ellen Carol. *Feminism and Suffrage: The Emergence of an Independent Women's Movement in America, 1848-1869.* (Cornell, 1978).

DuBois, W. E. B. *The Souls of the Black Folk.* (Greenwich, Connecticut, 1961).

Evans, Sara M. *Born for Liberty: A History of Women in America.* (New York, 1989).

Fehrenbacher, Don E. *Slavery, Law & Politics: The Dred Scott Case in Historical Perspective.* (New York, 1981).

Ferguson, H., ed. *Handbook on Human Rights and Citizenship.* (Albany, New York, 1981).

Fey, Harold E. and D'Arcy McNickle. *Indians and Other Americans: Two Ways of Life Meet.* (New York, 1959).

Flexner, Eleanor. *Century of Struggle: The Women's Rights Movement in the United States.* (Cambridge, Massachusetts, 1975).

Foner, Eric. *A Short History of Reconstruction, 1863-1877.* (New York, 1990).

Franklin, John. *From Slavery to Freedom: A History of Negro Americans.* (New York, 1967).

Gluck, Sherna Berger. *From Parlor to Prison: Five American Suffragists Talk About Their Lives.* (New York, 1976).

Grant, Joanne, ed. *Black Protest: History, Documents and Analyses, 1619 to the Present.* (New York, 1968).

Griffith, Elisabeth. *In Her Own Right: The Life of Elizabeth Cady Stanton.* (New York, 1984).

Gurko, Miriam. *The Ladies of Seneca Falls: The Birth of the Women's Rights Movement.* (New York, 1974).

Harding, Vincent. *There Is a River: The Black Struggle for Freedom in America.* (New York, 1981).

Hines, Paul D. and Leslie Wood. *A Guide to Human Rights Education.* Bulletin 43. (Washington, D.C., 1969).

Hoxie, Fredrick E., ed. *Indians in American History.* (Arlington Heights, Illinois, 1988).

Johansen, Robert W., ed. *The Lincoln-Douglas Debates.* (New York, 1965).

King, Martin Luther, Jr. *Why We Can't Wait.* (New York, 1964).

Kraditor, Aileen S. *The Ideas of the Woman Suffrage Movement, 1890-1920.* (New York, 1981).

Kraditor, Aileen S., ed. *Up From the Pedestal: Selected Writings in the History of American Feminism.* (Chicago, 1968).

Laqueur, Walter and Barry Rubin, eds. *The Human Rights Reader.* (Philadelphia, 1979).

Lengel, James G. and Gerald A. Dancer. *Law in American History.* (New York, 1987).

Levinson, Nancy Smiler. *The First Women Who Spoke Out.* (Minneapolis, 1983).

Lewis, Anthony. *Gideon's Trumpet.* (New York, 1964).

Linton, Calvin D., ed. *The Bicentennial Almanac: 200 Years of America.* (New York, 1975).

Low, W. Augustus and Virgil A. Clift., eds. *Encyclopedia of Black America.* (New York, 1981).

Martz, Carlton. *The Promise of Equality: Equal Rights and Equal Opportunity in American Life.* (Encino, California, 1977).

McNell, Andrew. *This Precious Heritage: Civil Rights in the United States.* (New York, 1988).

McNickle, D'Arcy. *Native American Tribalism: Indian Survivals and Renewals.* (New York, 1973).

Mendelsohn, Hack. *The Martyrs: Sixteen Who Gave Their Lives for Racial Justice.* (New York, 1966).

Milne, A. J. M. *Freedom and Rights.* (London and New York, 1968).

Milne, A. J. M. *Human Rights and Human Diversity: An Essay on the Philosophy of Human Rights.* (London, 1986).

Morris, Aldon. *The Origins of the Civil Rights Movement.* (New York, 1984).

National History Day 1991: Rights in History. (Washington, D.C., 1990)

Oates, Stephen. *Let the Trumpet Sound: The Life of Martin Luther King, Jr.* (New York, 1982).

Odegard, Peter H., Robert K. Carr, Marver H. Bernstein, and Donald H. Morrison. *American Government: Theory, Politics, and Constitutional Foundation.* (New York, 1961).

Odegard, Peter H. and Victor Rosenblum, eds. *American Government: Documents and Readings.* 2 vols. (New York, 1962).

Ortiz, Victoria. *Sojourner Truth: A Self-Made Woman.* (Philadelphia, 1974).

Palmer, R.R. "Man & Citizen: Application of Individual Rights in the French Revolution," *Essays in Political Theory Presented to G. H. Sabine.* (Port Washington, New York, 1972).

Ploski, Harry A. and James Williams, eds. *The Negro Almanac: A Reference Work on the African American.* (Detroit, 1989).

Pocock, J. G. A. *The Ancient Constitution and the Feudal Law: A Study of English Historical Thought in the Seventeenth Century; A Reissue with a Retrospect.* (Cambridge, England, and New York, 1987).

Prucha, Francis Paul. *The Indians in American Society: From the Revolutionary War to the Present.* (Berkeley, California, 1985).

Reid, John Phillip. *The Concept of Liberty in the Age of the American Revolution.* (Chicago, 1988).

Rio, Angel Ael. *Responsible Freedom in the Americas.* (New York, 1968).

Rosenbaum, Alan S., ed. *The Philosophy of Human Rights: International Perspectives.* (Westport, Connecticut, 1980).

Rubin, Louis D. Jr. *Virginia, A Bicentennial History.* (New York, 1977).

Sabine, George H. *A History of Political Theory.* (New York, 1961).

Schlesinger, Arthur M. Jr., ed. *The Almanac of American History.* (New York, 1983).

Schwelb, Egon. *Human Rights and the International Community.* (Chicago, 1964).

Schwoerer, Lois G. *The Declaration of Rights, 1689.* (Baltimore and London, 1981).

Segal, Geraldine R. *Blacks in the Law: Philadelphia and the Nation.* (Philadelphia, 1983).

Selby, Earl and Miriam Selby. *Odyssey: Journey Through Black America.* (New York, 1971).

Spicer, Edward H. *A Short History of the Indians of the United States.* (New York, 1969).

Sterling, Dorothy. *Black Foremothers: Three Lives.* (Old Westbury, New York, 1979).

Storing, Herbert J. *What Country Have I? Political Writings of Black Americans.* (New York, 1970).

Suter, Carol and Marshall Croddy. *American Album: 200 Years of Constitutional Democracy.* (Chicago, 1987).

Tankard, Alice. *The Human Family, Human Rights, and Peace: A Sourcebook for the Study and Discussion of the Universal Declaration of Human Rights.* (Detroit, 1973).

Thorne, Samuel E. et al. *The Great Charter: Four Essays on Magna Carta and the History of Our Liberty.* (New York, 1965).

Torney, Judith V. "The Elementary School Years as an Optimal Period of Learning about International Human Rights," in *Daring to Dream: Law and the Humanities for Elementary Schools.* (Chicago, 1980).

Trevelyan, George M. *The English Revolution, 1688-1689.* (London, 1973).

Tuck, Richard. *Natural Rights Theories: Their Origin and Development.* (Cambridge, England, and New York, 1979).

Tusa, Ann and John Tusa. *The Nuremberg Trial.* (New York, 1986).

Viorst, Milton. *Fire in the Streets: America in the 1960's.* (New York, 1979).

Washburn, Wilcomb E. *Red Man's Land/White Man's Law: A Study of the Past and Present Status of the American Indian.* (New York, 1971).

Williams, Juan. *Eyes on the Prize: America's Civil Rights Years, 1954-1965.* (New York, 1987).

Books for Young Readers

Aten, Jerry. *Our Living Constitution: Then and Now.* (New York, 1986).

Berry, Joe. *Every Kid's Guide to Understanding Human Rights.* (New York, 1987).

Commager, Henry Steele. *The Great Constitution: A Book for Young Americans.* (Indianapolis, 1961).

Cooke, Donald E. *America's Great Document: The Constitution.* (New York, 1973).

Cullop, Floyd G. *The Constitution of the United States: An Introduction.* (New York, 1984).

Findlay, Bruce and Esther Findlay. *Your Rugged Constitution.* (Palo Alto, California, 1969).

Fritz, Jean. *Shh. . .We're Writing the Constitution.* (New York, 1987).

Fritz, Jean. *The Great Little Madison.* (New York, 1989).

Fritz, Jean. *What's the Big Idea, Ben Franklin?* (New York, 1976).

Jenkins, Steve, L. Riekes, R. Goldman, and P. McKissack. *The Bill of Rights and You.* (St. Paul, 1990).

Kohn, Bernice. *The Spirit and the Letter: The Struggle for Rights in America.* (New York, 1974).

Lomask, Milton. *The Spirit of 1787: The Making of Our Constitution.* (Chicago, 1987).

Meltzer, Milton. *The Bill of Rights: How We Got It and What It Means.* (New York, 1990).

Morris, Richard B. *The Constitution.* (Minneapolis, 1985).

Olney, Ross R. and Patricia J. Olney. *Up Against the Law: Your Rights as a Minor.* (New York, 1985).

Prolman, Marilyn. *The Story of the Constitution.* (Chicago, 1969).

Sgroi, Peter. *Blue Jeans and Black Robes: Teenagers and the Supreme Court.* (New York, 1979).

Spier, Peter. *We the People: The Constitution of the United States.* (Garden City, New York, 1987).

Sterling, Dorothy. *Forever Free: The Story of the Emancipation Proclamation.* (New York, 1963).

Stevens, Leonard A. *How a Law is Made.* (New York, 1976).

Williams, Selma R. *Fifty-Five Fathers.* (New York, 1987).

Wise, William. *American Freedom and the Bill of Rights.* (New Haven, Connecticut, 1975).

Index

ACKNOWLEDGMENTS

This book has its origin in the Official 1991 Bicentennial Calendar, "The Bill of Rights and Beyond," published by the Commission on the Bicentennial of the United States Constitution in the fall of 1990 and, with the generous assistance of United Parcel Service, distributed to schools, colleges, public libraries, and other organizations in this country and around the world.

From the outset of its design, the calendar had been intended to serve as a teaching resource as well. Nevertheless, the enthusiasm and demand its distribution generated exceeded all expectations. Teachers, librarians, historians, attorneys, and others interested in the Constitution and the Bill of Rights expressed the wish that this wealth of material might be made available in more permanent form. The Commission, therefore, decided to adapt the calendar to a book format and to expand its material to include a larger number of historically significant dates, an extensive bibliography, and a collection of suggested teaching activities.

Many individuals contributed to the development of the original calendar and this book. The editors wish to acknowledge, in particular, Don Reilly, the calendar's chief editor, and the following people for their respective contributions: Burnett Anderson, Herman Beiz, Herbert Brownell, Stephen Burbank, Dustan Cross, Michael Feld, Charles Gittins, James Hutson, Ray Komai, Brian T. Kunzi, Kent Larsen, Thomas O'Connor, Donna Sicklesmith, Isidore Starr, Chuck Timanus, Denise Whelton, Steve Wilcox, Charles Alan Wright, and staff from the Library of Congress, the National Archives, the Government Printing Office, and the libraries of the New Executive Office Building, the General Services Administration, the United States Supreme Court, and the Department of Justice.

BOOK EDITORIAL

Editors:
Herbert M. Atherton
J. Jackson Barlow
Contributing Editor:
Stephen B. Sorensen
*Project Manager
and Photo Editor:*
Elisabeth M. Hartjens
Coordinators:
Patricia Andrews
Thomas J. Simon
Design:
David Moore
Calligraphy:
Julian Waters
Production:
Martha Chaconas
Typesetting:
General Typographers